MANAGING
SUPPLIER QUALITY

MANAGING SUPPLIER QUALITY

How to Develop Customer/Supplier Partnerships that Work

Roger L. Hale, Ronald F. Kowal,
Donald D. Carlton and Tim K. Sehnert

MONOCHROME
Press

Subsidiary of Gray Media, Inc.
Exeter, New Hampshire

© 1994 by Monochrome Press, Inc.

All rights reserved. This book or parts thereof may not be reproduced in any form without permission of the publisher.

ISBN: 1-882407-07-5

Library of Congress Catalog Card Number: 93-80938

Manufactured in the United States of America by
Maple-Vail Book Manufacturing Group

10 9 8 7 6 5 4 3 2 1

First Published in 1991 as *Made in the USA*
by Tennant Company, Minneapolis, Minnesota
Margaret Nelson, Editor
John H. Bush, Cartoonist
James Benoit, Original cover design
Kevin Pederson, Graphic Illustrator

Dedication

To all Tennant employees for their continued commitment to Tennant's Quest for Quality.

To all Tennant suppliers for their partnership and belief in excelling in all aspects of our business relationship.

To all Tennant customers throughout the world, who are the ultimate beneficiaries of our combined efforts.

Contents

Foreword by Tom Peters	vii
Introduction by Roger Hale	1
SECTION I: Improving Supplier Quality	3
Chapter 1: Why Supplier Quality is Important	5
Chapter 2: Purchasing's Leadership Role	13
SECTION II: Critical Success Factors	25
Chapter 3: Top-Down Emphasis on Quality	29
Chapter 4: Sense of Employee Ownership: A Corporate Team Approach	45
Chapter 5: Customer/Supplier Partnership	63
Chapter 6: Preventing Problems from Reaching the Customer	83
Chapter 7: Measuring and Reporting Quality	97
Chapter 8: Qualifying Suppliers	107
Chapter 9: Annual Business Management Sessions	121
SECTION III: Go For It!	133
Chapter 10: A Case Study	137
INDEX	143

Foreword

by Tom Peters

I feel like an old-time carnival barker on the midway: "And now, ladies and gents, for the ve-rry first time . . ." I think that's an accurate description of this marvelous book: *It's the first I've read solely devoted to the ins and outs of producers working with suppliers to achieve world-class quality.*

But then I've come to expect such firsts from Tennant, a company that lives and breathes quality — and is trying its darndest to get the rest of us to as well.

So, I like this all-important topic. Second, I like the timing. We've been in an appropriate dither about quality for a decade now, and have as a nation made giant strides — at the very least everyone in business is talking about quality. Our initial efforts focused on the firm itself, appropriately enough. ("Get your own house in order first" is always sound advice.) Supplier involvement has been a part of the best quality-improvement programs, but seldom front and center. Now the time has come, in the nineties, to move the suppliers' role in producer quality to the fore. After all, as Tennant points out, purchased components routinely make up 50 percent of the value of a manufacturer's product. (Our awesome exporter, Boeing, for example, only makes 100 percent of its aircrafts' wings — everything else, from avionics to engines to seats to the fuselage, is likely as not to come from a supplier.)

The third thing I like about this book is that it's written for you and me, not rocket scientists. There's a mention or two of Pareto analysis ("quality talk" for figuring out what few problems cause most of your quality debacles) and statistical process control — and they should be mentioned. But more important are homely checklists from the likes of Tennant's initial On-Site Supplier Assessment (one of eight parts of the company's supplier-qualification process): "Are measurements and goals [for the supplier's quality program] displayed?" "Are production operations promptly shut down when problems are discovered?" "Can [drawings and specifications] be electronically transferred to us?" And dozens more. And I love the common-sense form developed by Tennant Traffic Manager Teresa Frazee to evaluate freight carriers (see page 111); her sensible approach hits all the high points and the usually ignored items that go into a productive, lasting relationship with *any* supplier.

The seven key, heart-of-the-matter chapters each deal with an essential element of supplier-customer partnerships, from top-down management involvement and measurement to the conduct of annual review sessions. On the one hand, it adds up to a proven, no-nonsense, step-by-step guide to a supplier-customer revolution. But something more important lurks beneath the surface — and that "something" is not dwelled upon enough in these pages for my taste. You see, there's this attitude at Tennant (as there is at other nonpareil quality-star firms, such as textile-maker Milliken & Company). Tennant is really serious about this stuff. They live this stuff. After 10 years and enormous improvements, they picture themselves as no more than through the starting gate.

It boils down to the "World-Class Quality X-Factor." You see, I've reviewed all too many quality-improvement programs that are tops when it comes to charts, graphs, and techniques (I call them the "jargon junkies"); but quality is not in the soul of these outfits. It is at Tennant.

Perpetual quality improvement and a willingness to change everything and change it again are at the top of America's competitiveness agenda. Live it. Breathe it. Learn those painstaking lessons from this book. And enjoy. After all, there's nothing much more fun, not to mention profitable, than being associated with products and services that you can really brag about, whether you are an accountant, shipper, rubber-parts maker, or Minneapolis-based floor-cleaning equipment producer.

MANAGING
SUPPLIER QUALITY

Introduction

At Tennant, we're fortunate to have a reputation for manufacturing top-quality industrial and commercial surface maintenance equipment, supplies, and floor treating materials. As anyone in business knows, such quality takes effort.

One thing we've learned in our quest for quality is that Tennant products are only as good as what we put into them. Before we could be a top-quality supplier to our customers, we had to make sure we were dealing with top-quality suppliers ourselves.

In our earlier book, *Quest for Quality,* we discussed in some detail the changes we made internally to assure that quality comes first at Tennant. In this book we focus on a key external element: the supplier.

Very early in our quality-improvement efforts, which began in 1979, we realized that Tennant products are only as strong as our weakest supplier. Our purchasing people then turned their attention to improving supplier relationships. At first glance, it seemed like an easy enough thing to do: we figured we'd complain to the suppliers and they'd shape up.

Alas, it was not so easy. We found that developing quality suppliers — and quality supplier relationships — was far more complicated and time-consuming than we'd expected, yet also far more worthwhile for Tennant.

As we started to discuss various complaints and problems with our suppliers, we soon learned that Tennant was often a significant part of the problem. Our specifications weren't always clear, our standards were inconsistent, our communications were sometimes faulty, and we didn't know how to negotiate in the most professional and consistent manner. To improve our suppliers, we had to improve ourselves.

That process — of becoming the best buyers we can be and of helping our suppliers become the best suppliers they can be — has been one of the most rewarding experiences of our corporate life and of our quality effort at Tennant:

▶ We have become more professional in every way as we deal with suppliers.

- ► We have reduced the frustration that often characterized supplier/customer relationships.
- ► We have made enormous improvements in our product quality as a result of our suppliers' fine efforts.
- ► We have reduced our purchasing costs even as we've increased product quality.

When we began our quality work with suppliers, I was especially appreciative of our purchasing staff's pioneering efforts. To their great credit, they used me and other executives in a positive and constructive way. They called on us regularly to visit our peers at supplier companies, to greet them when they came for the rigorous all-day supplier conferences in Minneapolis, and to take a very active and energetic part in the all-supplier conferences that preceded our Zero Defects Days. It's been an interesting and enlightening experience for me. Without question, top management must set general direction for a quality effort and must support that effort with resources for training, technology, and people. At the same time, people throughout the organization must use top management in a constructive way and play that trump card when it will really help their cause.

We at Tennant are proud of our efforts to improve supplier quality. We are happy to share our experience, recognizing that this is just a beginning as we strive for perfection in our products and services.

Roger L. Hale
President and Chief Executive Officer
Tennant
Minneapolis, Minnesota

Section 1

Improving Supplier Quality

In recent years, it's become clear that quality is essential if American industry is going to regain and retain its competitive edge worldwide. Quality suppliers are a critical part of the quality mix. It's purchasing's responsibility to take the initiative in selecting and proactively developing those suppliers.

Chapter 1

Why Supplier Quality is Important

Our company's success — perhaps even its survival — depends on the quality of our suppliers. Sound far-fetched? Think about it. Products are only as good as the materials that go into them. In a sense, companies are only as good as their suppliers allow them to be.

In order to thrive into the next century, we all must produce quality goods and services. If we don't, we won't survive. Customers simply have too many options. Too many good companies in this country, Japan, Europe, and elsewhere are making things that work. No one has to settle for less.

Customers expect products to work 100 percent of the time, whether they buy one or one thousand. If our products don't work, customers may not always complain, but they won't always come back, either.

For most manufacturers, purchased components account for more than 50 percent of product cost. If your product has 10 components purchased from suppliers, and each piece has even a one percent failure rate, chances are your product won't always work, and not all of your customers will be satisfied.

With statistics like that, it's easy to see that quality suppliers are essential. To succeed in the marketplace, we all need suppliers who are committed to the quality of our products. We need *partners*. At Tennant, we've learned that successful partners: are *allies* in the struggle for market share, understand and *share our philosophy* of quality, and are willing to work toward *continuous improvement*.

Forming Ongoing Strategic Alliances with Suppliers

When Tennant began working on supplier quality, we weren't sure just where we'd find those wonderful suppliers who could be our long-term partners. We learned one thing fast: you don't find quality suppliers — you make them. By leveraging our purchasing authority and by training suppliers in what we expect, we've formed ongoing alliances with our suppliers based on what's good for Tennant as well as on what's good for them. No doubt you can do the same thing.

We've found that the greatest reward we can offer a good supplier is a long-term relationship, perhaps even a sole-source relationship. For example, National Purity has been Tennant's long-term sole source for certain chemicals and it's been good for everyone. As Jack Spillane, National Purity's president, says, "We don't start every week wondering if we have the business. We don't worry from day to day about losing business. We're tied right into Tennant's growth as long as we do what they need."

With a long-term commitment, suppliers can turn their attention away from finding business and toward servicing the business. They can confidently invest in research, equipment, and plant expansion. We count on our long-term suppliers to come up with ideas that will help us make our products better. Of course, buyers also enjoy tremendous benefits. As one of our procurement specialists has said, "It's kind of like a marriage. You stop shopping around and settle down for the long haul."

Being associated with a quality company can also help suppliers gain new customers. Duane Collins, executive vice president with Parker Hannifin, says he figures "if Parker can provide quality products as a sole-source supplier to Tennant, we can go out and say with confidence that we can do it for other customers."

No doubt, working together is a win/win situation for everyone involved.

Beat World-Class Competition with World-Class Quality

After World War II, American products were the epitome of quality worldwide. Everyone knew that American workmanship was best, American technology the most advanced, and American products were built to last. Nobody could compete with us.

But the market gradually changed until, by the early seventies, America's shiny reputation for workmanship had lost a bit of its luster. By the eighties, many American products were losing market share to foreign competitors — blown away first on price, later on quality. Of course, it's no secret who has taken the lead in consumer electronics, automobiles, computer technology, optics, and a variety of other products. Many American companies are struggling against Japanese competition; many are losing; some have already lost.

At the same time, countless U.S. companies are slapping their labels on imported goods, or buying components abroad for final assembly here.

But the Japanese aren't our only foreign competition. Many European companies — British petrochemicals, French computers, German manufacturing equipment — are going head-to-head with American companies in the domestic and international marketplace. Asian companies are also gaining a reputation for excellent work at a low cost. Korean televisions and consumer electronics are a major force. Singapore, Taiwan, Thailand, and many other Far East countries are shipping products worldwide. In just a few years, The People's Republic of China has become a major power in assembling low-cost consumer items.

To the south, Brazil is becoming an industrial power with domestic automobile, computer, and other manufacturing industries. Venezuela, Argentina, and their neighbors are entering the world market, rich in both labor and raw materials. As these countries continue to move from agricultural to industrial economies, they'll be even more competitive.

Such foreign competition threatens the whole U.S. economy. With every plant that closes, every product that dies, our economy's broad base narrows: we become more vulnerable to economic crisis; we have less control over our own markets; we lose ownership in our domestic resources.

Learning from the Competition

At Tennant, we believe in learning what we can from foreign competition and then focusing on making our own products as good as possible. For example, we met regularly with the Japanese Management Association for several years. We came to admire the Japanese focus on the long term. Japanese companies believe that their long-term focus gives them an edge over American companies in quality, service, and commitment.

It's a bit insulting to realize that the Japanese think their workers are better than ours. They think:

Japanese	Americans
"Sweat blood" over details	Don't sweat
Want to win the race	Want to be *in* the race
Hustle to get the job done	Plod along to fit in
Operate with a sense of urgency	Have a sense of complacency

In 1987, according to the *Wall Street Journal*, the Japanese owned 15 of the world's 25 most valuable public companies; only seven were American. Two years later Japanese control had increased dramatically: 19 companies were Japanese and only five were American. Of the world's 25 largest banks, the Japanese owned 15 in 1987, 17 in 1989.

Distressing as these numbers are, there's no secret to Japan's success. The Japanese are gaining a bigger share of the world market because consumers believe Japanese products are a better value than American products. Consumers believe they get more for their money; they believe Japanese companies are committed to quality. If American companies want to regain market share and improve the balance of trade, then we need to prove that we make quality products.

Recommitting to Quality

Despite the distressing problems of recent years, we think the future is wide open for American business. We don't support the doom and gloomers who think foreign industry is taking over the world. We believe in the ingenuity and resourcefulness of American business — that's one reason we're writing this book. We know there are many excellent companies in this country (we feel Tennant is one of them) and many more that simply need to recommit to quality.

❝ *Below is Tennant's quality policy reflecting our enhanced focus on meeting customer needs . . . we believe an emphasis on strategic quality will help us achieve our goals . . . keeping the customer as the focal point of all our efforts is the key to success."*
— Roger

Tennant Quality Policy
Commitment to Excellence

TENNANT *is committed to continuous improvement in identifying and satisfying worldwide customer needs at each and every point of contact.*

We believe that to achieve this continuous improvement we must strive for employee excellence, group excellence, and supplier excellence.

▶ **Achieving Individual Excellence for Each Employee**

Training and skill building
Recognition and respect for each employee
Universal involvement and empowerment

▶ **Achieving Group Excellence**

Communication
Effective, efficient, reliable processes for serving customers
Achieve comprehensive understanding of how each of our roles combines to meet customer needs

▶ **Achieving Supplier Excellence**

Partnership — mutually beneficial
Top Management Commitment — long-term relationship
Mutual Trust — open and candid communication

Future Challenges

Quality will be the basis of future American prosperity, but we'll have to get quality products to the market faster than we now think possible. The 1980s were the decade that rediscovered quality; the 1990s will be remembered for speed and response to the customer.

It can take many years to develop and introduce new products; in the United States we'll have to do better to compete in the world market. Some innovative American companies already have significantly shrunk that cycle through the use of computer-assisted design and computer-assisted manufacturing. AT&T, General Electric, and Motorola, among others, are cutting development time by 50 percent or more.

Computer-assisted design, from drawings to parts modeling, greatly shortens the design cycle. With automated manufacturing, companies can customize the product in whatever quantities are needed.

Quality suppliers are obviously a critical underpinning of this system. The speed and response required are possible only with suppliers who consistently meet *all* specifications. It's no luxury to establish a strategic alliance with your suppliers. It's the only way to compete in the world market.

Chapter 2

Purchasing's Leadership Role

Suppliers are purchasing's responsibility. In a well-run company, with well-developed customer/supplier relationships, the purchasing people will know individual suppliers as well as they know some of your other employees. Of course, suppliers will also have contact with others in your company — design and quality engineering, assembly, and/or materials control. But purchasing holds it all together, assuring that all aspects of the relationship are as effective as possible.

At Tennant, we used to make sure the supplier representative checked in with purchasing before talking with anyone else. Now — confident of our team approach — we know that it's really healthy to have our engineers and quality people talking back and forth with their supplier counterparts.

Our suppliers appreciate the openness, too. Loren Smith, president of Monona Wire, knows his people can talk to our engineers without going through red tape. "One thing about a good company, there's not a lot of politics, not a lot of hypersensitivity that someone's going to step onto your turf," Smith says. "At some companies, purchasing doesn't want you talking to anyone unless they're right there." It's a balance, to be sure: purchasing oversees the relationship without dictating every interaction.

Purchasing's role varies widely from company to company, depending in large part upon what top management delegates. It may range from a passive, nonstrategic role, simply reacting to input from other departments, to an active, strategic role. We support the strongest possible role for purchasing, but we know that our approach to developing quality suppliers can work in companies where purchasing is not particularly strong.

Five Stages in the Evolution of Purchasing

Basically, we see five progressive stages in the strategic development of the purchasing function. No department is probably ever "in" one specific stage; rather, it's usually in transition, with characteristics from two or more stages.

Understanding these stages is important because:
- ▶ You can recognize which stage your purchasing organization is in, and
- ▶ You can increase purchasing's impact in your company by developing skills to move to a higher stage.

We believe that a purchasing organization's stage of development clearly reflects that department's effectiveness in the company, perhaps even how competitive the company is in the world market. To make the best contribution, to have maximum effect on the bottom line, assess your department's present level of strategic integration and then plan to transform it to a higher stage.

The five stages differ in many ways, but perhaps most importantly they differ in their use of **strategy to define purchasing's role**. In the first, *rudimentary* stage, the purchasing department has no strategic direction — it merely processes purchase orders. In the second, *elementary* stage, purchasing continues to react, but uses technology to operate more efficiently. The third is the *fundamental* stage: purchasing knows it should be more proactive in company strategy, but is unwilling or unable to change. The fourth is the *advanced* stage: purchasing's strategy is closely directed by the firm's strategic direction. Fifth, in the *proficient* stage, purchasing helps formulate company strategy, recognized by top management as a valuable resource in maintaining competitiveness.

How the Stages of Purchasing Compare

These five stages reflect different types of purchasing organizations: the people in them have different types of goals, and the organizations make different contributions to the company. They are progressive stages, meaning that an organization can move through them in a certain order. Changing stages means reorganizing the way things are done. When a purchasing organization enters a new strategic stage, staff people think differently, act differently, and probably talk to different people than they did before.

Rudimentary Stage

At the rudimentary stage purchasing has no strategic direction: it reacts to the requests of others in the company. Personnel carry out clerical duties and exhibit little leadership. A supervisor who also has nonpurchasing responsibilities heads the department. Other things to look for at the rudimentary stage:
- ▶ Purchasing has little or no voice in choosing suppliers.
- ▶ Relations with suppliers may lack trust and harmony, and good relations may have no importance.
- ▶ The purchasing department has low visibility in the company and little communication with other departments, except for cutting purchase orders.
- ▶ Supplier selection is based on price and availability, not quality.

An example: CutRate, Inc., has cut costs by eliminating nine of the ten people in its purchasing department. The remaining purchasing agent simply distributes catalogs to each department; receptionists fill in order forms when not answering the phones.

Elementary Stage

Purchasing departments at the elementary stage are independent of the firm's competitive strategy. They may use innovative purchasing practices, but their role in the company remains reactive. Purchasing personnel have limited decision-making responsibility and limited leadership. The department may be headed by a supervisor reporting to a lower-level manager to whom purchasing is one of multiple responsibilities.

Companies operating at the elementary stage share the following characteristics:
- ▶ Purchasing may select from a list of suppliers; there's little or no competitive bidding.
- ▶ Quality awareness is surfacing.
- ▶ Relationships with suppliers are seen as short-term, not necessarily adversarial, but not as extensions of the company, either.

▶ More technology is used in purchasing support; there's systematic collection of supplier profile information, but little recognition of the importance of information systems in purchasing.

An example: Mo Jenkins is the purchasing agent at Murphy Conversion Vans. He points with pride to the computer programs that help him keep track of accounts. He has a subscription to *Purchasing* magazine. He reads up on all the latest purchasing techniques, and knows about JIT and quality circles. "It's too bad they don't keep up with these ideas in the front office," he says. "They could probably save some money."

Fundamental Stage

Purchasing departments at the fundamental stage are beginning to recognize the need to participate strategically in company decision-making. However, unable to change the traditional way that things are done, they can't take a proactive role. They recognize the need for supplier quality, collect supplier data, and may be headed by a middle-level manager who reports to a senior manager.

Characteristics of a company operating at the fundamental stage include:

▶ Competitive bidding is a primary means of supplier selection.

▶ Suppliers are seen as important in the organization; attempts are made to get them actively involved.

▶ Purchasing collects and uses data from other functions in managing supplier relationships.

▶ Personnel are beginning to recognize the need for integrated information within the company.

An example: Hometown Manufacturing Co. has instituted bidding procedures to streamline purchasing operations. They make an informal effort to work with friendly suppliers who cooperate to solve problems. The purchasing manager rates suppliers based on several quality criteria, including on-time delivery and percentage of defective products. She thinks it might be useful to have software to rate suppliers according to qualifying categories.

Advanced Stage

When purchasing is operating at the advanced stage, personnel know that they are strengthening the firm's competitive position. The manager and other department members make it their business to know the company's strategic plan and to operate within it. Purchasing officials interpret policy in making decisions. They may exhibit considerable leadership, with the head of purchasing reporting to a senior director or vice president.

At the advanced stage, purchasing departments share the following characteristics:

- ▶ Suppliers are carefully selected as a resource; they are trained in company expectations.
- ▶ People are considered a resource and are valued for their experience, motivation, and attitude.
- ▶ Purchasing monitors markets, products, and suppliers and analyzes them according to company needs.
- ▶ Management makes proactive use of information systems to strengthen relations with suppliers, tighten deadlines, and improve tracking.

An example: Circuit Master had to decide whether to fight foreign competition in the circuit breaker business or leave the industry. Financially it was a risk, but since Circuit Master had originated the concept and dominated the industry for years, they decided to stay in business. Management identified a strategic challenge: cut the time between order and delivery of customized product from three weeks to three days.

Corporate management radically redesigned their approach to manufacturing. Design engineers were directed to cut the inventoried parts list from 28,000 items to 1,275. They ordered purchasing to reduce the number of suppliers by 50 percent and work with remaining suppliers to establish 100 percent on-time delivery and zero defects. Sales learned how to enter detailed specs into a computer and the order-processing system

PEP GRID: Procurement Evolution Process

Characteristics	I Rudimentary	II Elementary	III Fundamental
Purchasing Role	Seen as efficient paper pushers. Reactive environment.	Use technology to automate and improve efficiency. Operate in reactive mode.	Recognize need to take more of a strategic role. Unable or unwilling to be proactive.
Supplier Selection	Suppliers chosen without purchasing involvement.	Select from list of known suppliers without competitive bidding.	Select suppliers based on competitive bidding.
Supplier Involvement	Nil. May be adversarial relation. Any supplier is expendable.	Short-term. Not extensions of your company, but mere suppliers of products/services.	Recognized as important. Take steps to involve them actively in company process
Supplier Quality Emphasis	None beyond filling the purchase order. Quality thought to be responsibility of others.	None beyond dealing with previous suppliers. Fast reactions to quality problems and efficient problem solving.	Recognize need; finding ways to implement. Collect data on measures of supplier quality, setting standards
Use of Information Systems (IS)	Clerical; seen as way to increase efficiency of administrative purchasing staff.	Problem tracking and reporting; build supplier profiles; limit use to support of purchasing.	Planning and con by management; other data source from within comp recognize need fo corporate informa systems.
Organizational Fit	Purchasing fragmented among several departments. Administrator reports to a supervisor.	Purchasing led by supervisor reporting to a manager with other responsibilities.	Purchasing led by mid-level manager reportin to higher manage

IV Advanced	V Proficient
Recognize need to take strong role in company; make the investments and commitments. Proactive contributions to the corporate strategic plan.	Significant contributor to corporate competitive position; seen as resource. Significant contributions to corporate strategic plan.
Select using formal process. Focus on key suppliers; input from nonpurchasing areas.	Select all suppliers using a formal process. Quality, design, procurement, and others on the sourcing team.
Early — before final specs. Early stages of customer/supplier partnership.	Formal, ongoing involvement in all aspects. Long-term partnerships with common objectives and goals; win/win environment.
Quality goals set with the supplier. Some inspection of product still routine. Ongoing communication about common goals and processes.	Aggressive, proactive supplier quality emphasis. No inspection necessary. Suppliers responsible for product quality. Intense assessments of suppliers at their sites.
Integrated internal systems to support strong supplier relationships; shorter response time used in JIT, etc. Multi-divisional integration of IS to support global sourcing strategies.	Use of EDI (electronic data interchange) to integrate supplier and purchaser IS; key competitive advantage seen in total IS across organizations; IS links to customers anticipated.
Purchasing led by a higher-level manager or a director reporting to a senior director or vice president.	Chief purchasing officer is at the vice presidential level; reports to president, CEO, COO, or a senior vice president.

was streamlined.

Iron Adams, punch press operator, explained their success: "The circuit breakers were only on the line for three days anyway back before we reorganized. We just cut out the paperwork time and eliminated delays due to late deliveries and nonconforming purchased parts. Now we're responsible for product quality and for scheduling our work. It means some extra involvement, but I'm glad to have a job. For a while it looked like we were going out of business."

Proficient Stage

At the proficient stage, purchasing is a full member of the corporate strategic team. Purchasing executives are important to the company. They formulate and implement corporate policy and strategic plans as peers with other departments; they make policy and exhibit executive leadership. A vice president who reports to a senior executive, such as the CEO, may head the department.

Companies with purchasing departments operating at the proficient stage generally share these characteristics:

- ▶ Supplier selection is based on formal criteria and evaluation by quality engineering, design engineering, and purchasing.
- ▶ Suppliers are seen as strong, full, long-term partners with common objectives and goals.
- ▶ Suppliers are completely responsible for quality, with no inspection at delivery.
- ▶ Information systems are central to managing purchasing.
- ▶ Supplier information systems become integrated with purchasing.

An example: Seymour Johnson started a computer company in his garage, wanting to build high-quality, superfast computers out of the best off-the-shelf parts available. He was successful and incorporated, appointed himself R&D director, and hired a CEO to run the company. The CEO had vice presidents of purchasing, marketing, assembly, and service, who worked together to set the company's strategic direction.

Evaluating Your Purchasing Organization

When we look at Tennant's purchasing, we review the characteristics of each stage and try to determine where our organization currently falls. We suggest you do the same. Your company may not fall clearly within one stage; most companies are in a process of evolution.

The ultimate goal is to move to the proficient stage, where purchasing is most proactive and most integrated into the overall corporate strategy and organization. Moving your company to a higher stage may take a long time — change happens slowly in corporate structures. But even a small step forward may have far-reaching effects. Plan for what you want for your company, and watch for signs of progress.

The grid on the preceding pages is a strategic roadmap. It summarizes the stages and highlights ways to assess your organization. Track your company's progress by following it on the grid.

Section 11

Critical Success Factors for Improving Supplier Quality

In our earlier book, *Quest for Quality*, we related how Phil Crosby asked us to list our ten best and our ten worst suppliers. As you may recall, we couldn't even begin to make that list; we didn't have the data. We didn't think in those terms. We thought we'd been doing a pretty good job and were embarrassed that we knew so little about the companies on which we depended. We decided we'd have to do better, and we have.

It was amazingly difficult to put together the seemingly simple information Crosby wanted. But it was worth the effort: as a result of gathering this data and building this list, we saw how important it was to keep data, including complete records on suppliers — delivery performance, reject rates, problem resolution information, and the like. Only with data can we know who is causing problems and who is providing quality service.

Since compiling that first list, we've developed very specific processes in working with purchased products and we've learned that quality suppliers behave in certain common ways. In the next seven chapters we'll discuss the "critical success factors" that we have identified as the foundation for working with our suppliers:

1. **Top-down emphasis on quality.** We want to be sure top management is committed to quality; this isn't something to delegate to second-level managers. Quality must be the customer's and supplier's central thrust, from the CEO on down.

2. **Sense of employee ownership: a corporate team approach.** Do corporate functions work together as an integrated team? Purchasing, design, production, marketing, and quality control should work in horizontally integrated product teams, not as separate units, vertically independent.

3. **Customer/supplier partnership.** At Tennant, we address problems by working with the supplier. A win/win customer/supplier partnership means the parties trust each other and work toward mutual success.

4. **Preventing problems from reaching the customer.** Suppliers should work closely with us during the design stage

of our parts to help us meet tough customer quality and reliability requirements. Supplier/customer communication and cooperation must begin early in the product development process and should continue throughout production.

5. **Measuring and reporting quality.** Suppliers should measure quality, reliability, and delivery by continually collecting, analyzing, and reporting data. As a customer, Tennant gives suppliers frequent, precise, and detailed feedback on their performance.

6. **Qualifying suppliers.** Suppliers should meet qualification criteria within a specified time and maintain it during the entire relationship. They should meet expectations.

7. **Annual Business Management Sessions.** We expect suppliers to be prepared to meet with us annually to candidly explore common issues. That candor and commitment is basic for the kind of supplier relationships we're after at Tennant.

Wouldn't it be convenient to have at your fingertips a "critical success factor" directory that you could refer to as a roadmap to improving supplier quality? The next seven chapters provide the background we used in shaping Tennant's supplier quality emphasis, which has helped Tennant establish an international reputation for quality. We hope that you will find the factors to be a useful road map in your journey toward continuous supplier-quality improvement.

Chapter 3

Top-Down Emphasis on Quality

The first step in improving supplier quality is to *involve the supplier's top management*. Whether you're a large or small part of their business, whether you've done business with them for many years or just a few months, it is crucial to involve the very top, because it's top management that makes the kinds of commitments you're after.

Getting Started

Our supplier executives have very busy schedules, and we were nervous about making that first phone call to invite them to individual meetings. We found a most effective strategy to involve upper management directly in our meetings: we simply — and honestly — told them that we were paring down our list of suppliers. "We have a lot of problems using your parts," we said. "We hope you can make the meeting to discuss some strategies for improvement."

Most of the people we invited responded well to that angle. Once at the meeting, we explained our quality approach and they pledged their cooperation. From the beginning some saw an opportunity to improve their company's commitment to quality; others came to understand that opportunity.

We held our first meeting in October of 1980; it took us a year to do that first group of 10. We met with 15 supplier executives the second year, 25 the third.

A few of those suppliers didn't send their top executives to our meetings, nor did they make a commitment to our business. Perhaps they were too busy; perhaps they didn't want us to influence their internal operations. Over time, we've lost touch with them.

Large Companies Are Surprisingly Receptive. In the beginning, we weren't sure how effectively our simple approach would work in reaching the top echelons of the huge companies with whom we deal. For example, we bought 300 engines a year from Ford Motor Company — obviously not a big customer. We were afraid they wouldn't even talk to us.

Jumping In. We decided to try to reach the top guy at Ford and started making phone calls. We talked to our sales rep,

> *We're confident that the quality improvement processes we have in place with suppliers are working ... the results speak for themselves ... our ultimate goal is to have suppliers take complete ownership of the quality of parts they supply ... enabling us to discontinue incoming inspection altogether."*
> — Ron

Tennant Purchased Part Reject Rate
(INCOMING INSPECTION)

LOTS REJECTED

- '81: 7.3%
- '83: 2.8%
- '85: 1.9%
- '87: 1.8%
- '89: 1.5%
- '91 Projected: 1.0%

our sales rep's boss, and his boss. It took seven or eight phone calls just to understand Ford's organizational structure. Finally we reached the top person in industrial engines: Bob Donnelly.

We invited him to Minneapolis. He said no, but invited us to Detroit. We went, a bit overwhelmed about going to corporate headquarters. We didn't expect much to happen, but decided to make the effort. We gave our one-hour presentation about Tennant's commitment to quality.

Fortunately, Bob is committed to the customer and to improvement and is in a position to make things happen.

Why We Made the Phone Call. Back then, we were using four or five engine suppliers and had to adjust or repair more than half the engines we bought. That extra work was costing us money, and we knew the problems were preventable.

Today our engines work right out of the box. We got Ford's attention and we've kept it. John Schlegel, power products manager at Ford, says frankly that Tennant played a key role in getting Ford involved in quality. "We're proud of our quality but, quite honestly, Ford didn't embrace some of Tennant's concepts until a year or two after that first meeting," John notes. "They were blunt with us. They said 'We are reducing our supplier base to improve quality. If you want to be one of our suppliers, you'll have to improve.' It was strong stuff."

John remembers when Ford vice president Joe Kordik came out from Dearborn to our Zero Defects Day in 1985; he was so impressed with Tennant's commitment "from the hourly employees through top management that he came back and used Tennant as an example of what we should do."

Securing Commitments

In the initial meeting, we know it's vitally important to have Tennant's top management meet our supplier's top management, one-on-one. After making our presentation about improving supplier quality, we ask for commitment on the spot. We ask them to set goals and we work with them to identify those goals. And we give them our *Quest for Quality* book as a reminder of our total commitment to quality.

> *It was a matter of defining and communicating what we needed ...Ford proved responsive ... now, years after the published article on the special celebration, we can still count this as one of our many success stories ... and while we're proud of that, both Tennant and Ford recognize that continuous improvement must be pursued."*
> — Don

Ford strikes new bargain with Tennant

On January 13, 1988, Tennant celebrated the beginning of a new partnership with Ford Motor Company. Just two weeks prior to that, Ford began supplying Tennant with new 1.1 and 1.3 litre engines manufactured at Ford's Valencia, Spain, plant. Tennant's senior procurement specialist, Rick Anderson, explains, "The new Valencia engine offers Tennant several benefits, including lower cost, higher quality and reliability, and direct shipment from the factory."

Why the celebration? Because Ford and Tennant have agreed to work together to solve any production problems. Of this new partnership, Dave McKercher, OEM sales manager for Ford, says, "We have always enjoyed a good business with Tennant, and we think that we are serving up a newer and better-quality engine than we have had before."

McKercher was referring to the old Kent engine, supplied to Tennant in the past from Ford's Kent, England, plant. Ford is phasing out this engine and began supplying the new, improved Valencia engine to Tennant on December 13, 1987.

The January 13 celebration marked Ford's and Tennant's commitment to putting out a quality product together. Doug Hoelscher, Tennant vice president, reassured employees from Manufacturing, Engineering, Purchasing and Final Test gathered together for this occasion that, "Ford has agreed to work with us on any problem that comes up, and they have agreed to solve that problem both in Detroit and in the plant." He added that, "We still need your help and input when we do run into problems. Only by working together will this become a successful venture for Ford and Tennant."

Supplier Commitment. After we met with one supplier's top management, they called all their people together to discuss expectations. They set goals and mapped out the steps necessary to reach them, as we'd asked them to do. They also ordered 150 copies of Crosby's book (this was back before we'd written our first book) for key employees, *and* tested them on it.

The point: we had made an impression. We'd insisted on having top management involved and we'd clearly outlined our needs. We asked them to work with us on our quality goals and we made a commitment to work with them. As a result of our joint efforts, we got better and better.

We have seen continuous improvement from our suppliers. They have an ongoing relationship with us that they can count on. We've all benefited.

Long-Term Commitment. We set up each supplier's quality improvement program in three-year increments, if possible. Once a supplier has met with us and agreed with our goals, we commit to work with them for up to three years. We aren't alone in making multiyear commitments. One of our suppliers just got a $300 million contract with the Pentagon that stretches out eight years. The purchasing people in the Defense Department have recognized that they don't need to shop around; they make commitments to suppliers just as they expect suppliers to make commitments to them.

Top-Management Commitment. Look for commitment by top management on both sides of the partnership — your own and your supplier's. At Tennant, Roger became committed to quality after visiting Japan and consulting with Phil Crosby. Other Tennant executives supported him based on their independent conclusions. We were faced with overseas competition, and we wanted to beat it.

If you find top-management commitment to quality in your supplier, and you also find it in your own top management, you have a crucial element of success already in place. If commitment at the top is missing, your first task is to build it. Commitment to quality is not a matter to be delegated to subordinates.

Top-Management Involvement Is Essential

If someone at Tennant needs to talk to our top contact at Ford, we have our vice president make the call. We work through equal levels. This telephone route gives us flexibility and immediacy in dealing with tough issues as they come up.

Keeping Top Management Involved. Once we have top management's attention, we keep them involved. We've found several things especially helpful, including:

- Annual Business Management Sessions
- On-site visits
- Zero defect days
- Quality reporting

Whatever you decide to do, do it with zest. Pomp and circumstance add a lot: publicize these events, whoop it up, get people involved and excited, and let everyone in the plant know what is happening. These things have worked for us. You'll no doubt have other ideas on how to involve top management in improving supplier quality.

Annual business management sessions will be examined in detail in a later chapter so we won't discuss them here. However, let's look briefly at other ways to involve top supplier management.

Defining On-Site Visits

On-site visits are another key aspect of our supplier quality emphasis. As with the annual business management sessions, the most important factor is having the top people there. In fact, if they aren't present for the on-site visit, cancel the meeting. Reschedule it for another day, and be explicit about time and place. You *must* meet with the supplier executives at least briefly; you can't have a successful visit unless you do. As we've said before, they're the people who can make quality happen. They set the tone for their company.

Make It Fun. We don't spend a lot of money, but we like to bring along little souvenirs to help our suppliers remember us. We hand out a little knife that says "slicing defects." We give

Closing Loops

Hustle, spirit, and energy characterize Parker Hannifin, a Tennant supplier of hydraulic hoses, fittings, and quick couplers for more than 20 years.

In addition to top-quality products and 100 percent on-time delivery, there is something else that earned Parker Hannifin their sole-source role with Tennant. They also have an excellent attitude about how to treat their customers — something Tennant values and appreciates.

One of the reasons Parker Hannifin has earned this distinction is their performance. During the last three years, for example:

- On-time deliveries have been at or near 100 percent. They send us over 2,000 shipments every six months.
- In 1989, of the approximately 250,000 parts used in assembly, 121 were rejected because of defects. That's 4.8 defective parts per 10,000.

During a recent business management session at Parker Hannifin's Cleveland, Ohio office with President and CEO Paul Schloemer and others, we showed them the 4.8 defects per 10,000 statistic, which indicates pretty good performance, but Schloemer had a different response. He said, "Yeah, but you pay to get them **all** right, don't you?" Schloemer then turned to his vice presidents and plant managers and asked, "Have we isolated those 121 problems yet and closed the loop on them?"

It was a clear message to us and to his people about how important quality is to Parker Hannifin and how important Tennant's business is to them.

When we first began sharing this story, many people found it hard to believe that the CEO of a $2.5 billion company would actually meet with us, a customer. We were told that this was simply a stroke of luck and not likely to happen again.

Well, they were right. In a later meeting, Schloemer wasn't available to see us. So, his boss came instead — Patrick Parker, Chairman of the Board. Imagine that!

— Don

away our books. We look for any little thing that will sit on their desk and say, "Tennant Quality." There are hundreds of "leave-behinds" you can order — clocks, plaques, flashlights. Have fun with it.

Go In a Group. Have your quality engineers come along to meet their supplier counterparts. Sometimes it's helpful to bring along assembly people, shop supervisors, designers. Take the opportunity to review their quality results, share notes, and make it a big event. On-site meetings should be important and memorable occasions because they are a major step toward improving your supplier's behavior. Commemorate the events. Make an impact on the people involved.

When Tennant was exploring a sole-source relationship with Parker Hannifin, we took a number of our people to their plants. Veteran assembler Don Steile went along, looking for ways to train our people in attaching Parker's hoses. "It's hard to explain, but it really made a difference going out there," Don says. "You see their plant, you get to know them a bit. Somehow, you're more able to ask questions; they're more willing to answer. You feel like you get to know them."

ZD Days

Zero Defects Day is Tennant's festival of recognition for employees, suppliers, and everybody involved with quality. It's held every few years after months of planning by a special ZD Day committee.

ZD Day is also an excellent way to involve supplier top management in improving quality; it's our chance to show suppliers how Tennant's quality commitment works internally. Purchasing agent Jane Angell looks at it like this: "Once a supplier sees the whole company taking a day to celebrate quality, there's no doubt what we stand for."

Group problem-solving displays are an example of ZD Day highlights. Employees turn out wearing the company colors or bedecked with posters, balloons, or other attention-getting devices to document and promote the successes of the many small groups that knit our company into a closely functioning unit.

Employees get a chance to talk about what they've done to improve quality and learn what others have done as well. One group came up with several improvements for a new machine, making it an exceptional product. Another group, called "Stop Waste at Tennant," declared themselves a SWAT team and turned out in uniform. Still another team did a skit where Sir Q guarded the factory gate. As part of the day, we all sign pledges renewing our commitment to quality. It's a proud and happy day for everyone involved.

Groups disband once they solve the problem, but the spirit that comes from working together — and from celebrating at an event like ZD Day — lives on and motivates us to do our best.

In conjunction with ZD Day, Tennant hosts a supplier fair, bringing in all suppliers for a formal session on quality improvement. For example, one year Ford's Joe Kordik was our keynote speaker. He spoke about how "At Ford, Quality

Tennant shares first ZD Day experience with Midwest Rubber

On December 1, Midwest Rubber celebrated their first Zero Defects Day. As part of their celebration, all 31 employees visited Tennant to see how their products (squeegees and flexible hoses) are used in our equipment.

During their Tennant visit, Midwest Rubber employees toured Plant I, saw their products demonstrated on our Model 530E and the Vicuna, and signed a quality pledge. They also saw our *Quest for Quality* and supplier quality videos.

According to their president, Chuck Anderson, Midwest Rubber takes our supplier quality program very seriously and has indicated their commitment to becoming a qualified supplier by having their first Zero Defects Day. Anderson has attended several supplier quality programs at Tennant in the past and uses Tennant as a role model in developing a quality process at Midwest Rubber.

> *We're a bit overwhelmed at how receptive our suppliers are in participating in our ZD Days . . . it's also enlightening and flattering for us to be a part of some suppliers' own ZD day celebrations . . ."*
> — Tim

Suppliers' Reactions to ZD Day Reflected in Letters

I can't tell you how impressed we were with the enthusiasm all your employees exhibited toward such an excellent program. It is obvious that it has and will continue to pay dividends. There were many thought-provoking ideas throughout the agenda which have caused us to review our operations for quality improvements . . .

We look forward to doing our part to nurture and improve the excellent relationship between our companies.

— **Foundry Supplier**

Zero defects has taken a lot of work at the Tennant Company and at our company, but it has been well worth it. Our percentage of zero defects is currently at 99%! We will continue to strive for zero defects and start tackling some of our other problem areas.

— **Hydraulic Component Supplier**

For me it was an impressive and inspiring day . . . Impressive because of the significant improvements you and your company have accomplished in the areas of defect detection and prevention over the last two years.

I also found it to be an inspiring day because of the overall management commitment and the total employee attitude that was prevalent wherever we went throughout the day.

We are proud to be a major supplier, and contributor, to your extraordinary success, and we will rededicate our effort to continue to supply to you well-designed and conforming products.

— **Steering Component Supplier**

is Job One." We also had several booths displaying joint Tennant/supplier problem-solving groups. Suppliers also sign a formal pledge of quality. By celebrating our accomplishments together, we enhance our relationship with our suppliers. They truly feel a part of Tennant.

Quality Reporting

Written feedback, both positive and negative, is another effective way to get top management's attention. At Tennant, we accumulate data on accepted incoming lots, zero defects, reliability, and on-time delivery. Every six months we send a performance report to our suppliers' top management, reminding them of our seemingly uncompromising tough goals and comparing their actual performance against them. As appropriate, we send a cover letter commending them for superior performance or pointing out where improvement should be made. We also ask them to submit improvement goals for the next reporting period.

The letters make a big impact. Don Zito, president of Parker Hannifin's fluid connectors group, still remembers the day he got a letter from Tennant's Procurement Specialist Rich Carlson telling him Parker had become a qualified supplier. "It wasn't really a good day for me and then I got that letter — the nice gold label. I thought, 'My God, this is fantastic'. It made my day," Don recalls. "Actually it made my whole week."

Impact of Quality Reporting. Don's not the only executive who's been so enthusiastic. These reports have a tremendous impact on supplier performance and attitude and they're a valuable trouble-shooting tool. Suppliers recognize the data as significant to everyone in their organization: labor, management, and administration. When they send us replies, they've usually "copied" a long list of internal people, reflecting the broad impact of their commitment to Tennant quality.

Certificates Draw a Large Response. Along with our quality reports, we send certificates printed on metallic gold, fluorescent green, or blaze orange paper highlighting the supplier results. The certificates elicit emotional responses, ranging from dewy pride to stark terror, with messages such as:

> *Supplier Quality updates are really just a report card on their past performance . . . areas for improvement are highlighted . . . we also recognize good performance."*
> — Don

- ▶ **"Congratulations!** What a fantastic accomplishment — your excellent performance has earned you our fully QUALIFIED SUPPLIER status. Welcome to this elite group."
- ▶ **"Your improvement is showing!** While you remain a CONDITIONALLY QUALIFIED SUPPLIER, you're making positive progress toward reaching the elite status of a fully qualified supplier. A little more effort and you'll make it — keep trying."
- ▶ **"Declining performance warning!** Did you know that your level of performance continues to label you as only a CONDITIONALLY QUALIFIED supplier, that you're showing no improvement, and that your performance has actually gotten worse? What are you significantly planning to do about it and how can we help?"

We put great effort into providing this level of quality reporting, but the work is essential and the payoff is terrific. We need to be demanding in our analysis, establishing and enforcing our standards and expecting our suppliers to meet them. We take risks in evaluating the people we deal with and in giving them negative feedback where warranted. But it's the only way we know to eliminate defects and create a top quality, world-class product.

Summary

At Tennant, we've found four key ways to involve our suppliers' top management in improving quality. **Annual Business Management Sessions** allow us to look at all aspects of our business relationship. **On-site Visits** enable us to make a lasting impression on our suppliers, and are cancelled if top management isn't present. **Zero Defects Day** helps everybody associated with the product — both suppliers and employees — to understand and celebrate the importance of their efforts on the quality team. **Quality Reporting** reflects supplier performance as well as our own ongoing determination to uphold quality standards. Securing a commitment from top management is essential — by involving them, we assure a quality commitment throughout the supplier company.

Chapter 4

Sense of Employee Ownership: A Corporate Team Approach

A visitor to Japan, riding the airport bus from Narita airport to downtown Tokyo at 9:00 p.m. on a weeknight, gets the distinct impression that Japanese offices work two shifts. As the bus drives past mile after mile of well-lit office buildings, the visitor sees people hard at work, and almost every desk occupied. The next day, the visitor is told that people in Japan work a standard 9-to-5 day. However, when 5:00 p.m. rolls around, he notes that no one goes home.

At 6:00 p.m. employees gather briefly in the lunch room for ramen and tea. At 9:45 chimes sound to indicate that the building will close in 15 minutes. At 9:55 employees begin to stir toward the door, and at 10:00 p.m. a polite and smiling man with a broom waits for the last person to get off the elevator so he can lock up and sweep the lobby.

When the visitor asks if the building will be open on the weekend so he can prepare for a Monday presentation, he's told that it probably will. At 10:00 a.m. Saturday the visitor finds almost every desk occupied. He's a bit embarrassed to be the last one in.

When he leaves at 3:00 p.m., half the desks are still occupied. The insurance offices upstairs and the import/export business downstairs are similarly occupied — in fact, few offices are dark. Everybody's working — at terminals, in meetings, on the phone — rounding out their 70-hour work weeks.

After returning home to the United States, the visitor learns that Japanese workers are loathe to come home in the daylight because the neighbors will think they aren't *important* to their company. They'll "lose face." Their families will be embarrassed.

Every Employee Is Important

In many U.S. companies, employees don't consider themselves important. They "fill slots." They may think that only the VIPs matter.

One reason that Japanese products are winning international quality competition is that they're made by people who consider themselves important. They expect to be important to their company. They feel a sense of community within the firm. They belong. Each worker feels responsible for product quality. This *sense of employee ownership* is the second critical success factor we've found essential in quality suppliers. All the suppliers' employees should recognize how their work affects others; what they do and who they are is vitally important to their company and to delivering quality products.

At Tennant, we believe all employees are important and we're determined to make them feel that way. We want our suppliers to learn from us.

For example, we get our assemblers involved with new products in the prototype stage. We want their opinions. Will it work? Can it be assembled this way? This is a relatively recent change for us. For years we manufactured products for our international division without ever asking what was needed in Europe. Everything had to be reworked, costing time and money. Finally, well into our quality emphasis, our European colleagues told us we were their worst supplier. That's when we took our own advice to heart, striving to provide our international customers with the same quality that we expect from our suppliers.

Frans de Bekker, quality assurance manager for our Netherlands division, recalls how bad the problems were. "Everything was designed in inches, while Europeans use metrics. They were designed for U.S. sources so nothing manufactured in Europe fit. It was a mess."

Working Together

Establishing a sense of employee ownership begins with company executives. Top management can acquire skills and attitudes that will naturally lead to a "do-it-right-the-first-time" mentality among employees. The result: increased productivity and quality. Early in our quality emphasis, our employees wore buttons proclaiming, "It's up to me."

It's essential for executives to master and implement the concept of *a product-focused team corporate structure.* Simply put, that's teamwork. The goal is to have small groups of employees working together to design products, solve problems, brainstorm about new products — the list is endless. These small groups may be temporary or permanent. They exist horizontally — at top management levels, middle management, and in the shop. They also exist vertically — executives and machine operators; engineers, purchasers, and quality control; sales, designers, and assemblers. The key word is function: the small groups are *functional teams*.

You don't need to reorganize your company to make functional teams work. The organization chart, office assignments, and job duties need not change. However, other changes are crucial, including:

► Training all employees
► Building employee respect
► Recognizing accomplishment
► Mentoring small groups
► Examining past culture and environment

Let's look briefly at each of the changes.

Training All Employees. For small groups to be successful, all employees need training, beginning with management and extending throughout the company. Listening, problem solving, and planning skills all improve with training; they help employees work in small groups and they also transfer to job skills. Other small group process skills involve understanding yourself, understanding others, communication styles, and building self-esteem.

We've spent training time on all these skills. Roger mandates the training and the emphasis pervades our company. Oh, a few supervisors may grumble now and then about lost work time, but they don't grumble very loud. They know that education — training — is vital. As a sign in our vice president's office reads, "If you think education is expensive, try ignorance."

In addition to basic group skills, improving supplier quality requires training in such technical skill areas as statistical quality control, Pareto diagrams, cause and effect diagrams, reliability, blueprint reading and torque training. We also encourage cross-training in other skills, so employees have the skills to do what needs to be done. For example: machine operators may try their hand at inspecting; a welder may spend time in shop floor control; industrial engineers may work in purchasing. As employees improve in one area, they can work on another. To be successful, quality improvement programs must include skills training.

Building Employee Respect. Imagine a small group in which the company CEO sits down to discuss new product design with engineers, sales reps, and assemblers. In most companies, such a group would sound more like a public relations photo opportunity than a working committee: why would the design ideas of an assembler and sales rep interest the CEO and designer?

We focus on listening to employees and letting them become creatively involved. For example, industrial engineers suggested a $120,000 reorganization of the welding area. Top management said no. A few years later, the operators (those most immediately involved with welding) came up with a substantially lower figure and got what they wanted. If the welders hadn't cared, hadn't been concerned about quality, efficiency, and productivity, they wouldn't have made the effort. But they did care — they knew they were important. And they knew that the company respected them enough to listen.

Recognizing Accomplishment. Recognition builds trust and makes employees feel important. The more you recognize quality performance and outstanding accomplishment, the better that performance will be. Not only are you reinforcing positive behavior by recognizing it, you're also educating employees about the behavior you want. Since most workers want to succeed at their jobs (both because they need the income and because they want the satisfaction of doing well), they'll follow the positive behavior modeled for them.

Zero Defects Day, discussed earlier, is an example of a recognition event for all employees; Tennant's World Class Quality and Productivity Conference is another. We invite our suppliers to participate in these recognition events — both to see Tennant's enthusiasm for quality and as a model for their own quality programming.

" *Diamond-studded rings, 10 karat gold pins, and plaques are given to our employees as recognition . . . this program's success was the driving force behind our supplier recognition process . . . and the value suppliers place on formal recognition has turned out to be far beyond our wildest expectations."*
— Tim

Formal Quality Recognition
Individuals & Groups

Objective: To recognize employees who demonstrate outstanding quality performance.

Individuals are recognized annually, groups semi-annually, based on the following criteria:

▶ Continuous superior performance in doing work right the first time over a minimum of one year.

▶ Cooperative, positive approach to problem solving.

▶ Taking the initiative in corrective action to solve problems.

▶ Setting quality goals and demonstrating high-level effort to attain goals.

▶ Communications and other actions to support the Quality Program.

> **❝** *We have a lot of fun with the Koala T. Bear award at Tennant. This is a reprint of some recent publicity about the Bear . . . we support any type of recognition that rewards good performance . . . and it works with suppliers, too."*
> — Ron

The Bear Is Here for You!

Everybody knows me. Even from 50 feet away. I dress differently from most and never talk. But other things I do speak more loudly than words. I'm Koala T. Bear, and this year I've celebrated my fifth anniversary. In that time I've been more places and hugged more people than I can count! (Nearly 1000.)

As you may remember, I am part of your quality recognition program. I represent the award employees get when they:

- Consistently meet job standards
- Have a positive work attitude
- Put forth extra effort in output, quality, or efficiency.

When I first started making calls, people weren't so sure what to think of me. Some laughed, some had real tears in their eyes, and some were downright embarrassed. My committee members were sensitive to these feelings and for a while sent me to Arizona for retirement. But not for long . . .

Employees missed me too much! In less than three months, I was back making presentations, giving those cute little stuffed bears to people, and awarding them bear pins. No one knows the exact number of bears I've awarded, but in 1989 I gave out 60 awards to Tennant Company employees locally and 45 awards to field employees. (They love me in the field, too.)

Don't think it hasn't been fun. I have lots of good memories. Every time I make an appearance at the company picnic or during ZD Day celebrations I get that shot in the arm that keeps me going. Kids really love me. Some adults go crazy over me, too! Even strangers stop when they see me driving down the freeway on my way to Plant II.

I've been known to surprise many people. On one occasion I awarded a bear to two people who had nominated each other for the award. Imagine their surprise! And another time I made a special trip to a Steak and Ale Restaurant to present my award. I've even presented the bear to President Roger Hale, who, by the way, seemed quite pleased. I must say that I have no favorites — I love you all!

And of course I've changed over the years. Already I've worn out one bear suit and have had to order another. My little stuffed bears have changed, too — from shaggy to smooth. Don't tell anyone, but I even gave out a defective bear one time. One of its ears (poor thing) was sewn on backwards. With a little rework, however, my customer was soon satisfied.

Lots of employees have walked in my shoes, so they know how I feel about these award presentations. I loan my suit out every month to those eager employees who want to know what it's like to surprise, embarrass, or tantalize their coworkers.

I owe all you employees a lot of credit for accepting me as I am and even hugging me, for crying out loud. Yes, some people get so excited that they just can't resist putting their arms around my furry person. But we bears need our hugs, too. So keep those bear hugs coming.

And don't forget to nominate someone who deserves me for the next round of Koala T. Bear awards. Nomination forms are available in bins at all building locations and in the field.

Remember, this bear's for you!

Tennant also has two annual, company-wide formal recognition events for small group achievement — periodic festivals that celebrate small group accomplishments and recognize employees in the presence of important others including family and friends.

In addition, several outstanding individuals are formally recognized once a year at the annual Award of Excellence dinner where they receive a plaque and a diamond-studded ring. For example, Bob Milford of Tennant's stockroom got the award because he takes a proactive approach to his job — alerting people to damaged shipments and shortages, always having the information or part they need. Rick Anderson in purchasing received the award as a result of his outstanding performance in developing effective supplier relationships, among other accomplishments. The four of us have also been honored to receive the award.

Another popular formal recognition at Tennant is the teddy bear presented monthly by a costumed character named Koala T. Bear. Peers nominate employees who: consistently meet job standards; have a positive work attitude; and expend extra effort in output, quality, or efficiency.

The Koala T. Bear award is very popular among employees, both to give and to get. Different employees don the costume to make the awards and present them in a variety of places — the office, at a restaurant, even during a meeting. Employees react strongly, often hugging the bear, laughing, or crying. With such an emotional impact, people remember the award for a long time. Roger fondly recalls the day he accompanied K.T. Bear on her rounds. "No matter who we are and what we do, we like recognition for doing a good job," Roger says. "I once saw genuine tears come to the eyes of a rather burly and rough-n-tough member of our field service crew when he received one of those cute little stuffed animals."

Mentoring Small Groups. Small groups about quality and productivity may come together spontaneously or be put together by top management. In either case, they meet sometimes to solve an existing problem, other times with some other specific mission in mind. Management commitment and participation — full participation, including time, budget, and personal involvement — are critical for small groups to succeed.

When a company is trying to change its culture, each small group needs a champion who can mentor the group and who has the power to overcome organizational barriers. Often the mentor makes the difference in helping the group accomplish its objectives.

Tennant's top managers spend two to four hours a week working with two or more small task-oriented groups. The executives benefit because they keep in touch with the employee mood and attitude; middle managers learn to recognize small incremental gains toward company goals such as zero defects; employees learn the importance of establishing quality and productivity goals and objectives. Ron mentored a welding department group that reduced the cost of quality 40 percent in one year, while increasing efficiency.

Examining Past Culture and Environment. It requires change to integrate a company's organizational structure — to establish teamwork and worker ownership in the company's success. Top managers must identify where the company is and where they want it to go. The first step is a candid look at the present environment.

For example, back in 1979, we had an excellent company. We had low turnover, promotion from within, first-name relations. Executives spent time on the shop floor; they considered themselves head of the Tennant family. But they knew we had to get even better.

In 1981, after two years of small groups, top management made some important discoveries about Tennant's culture and environment. Ron recalls: "We found that we were not very good listeners; we were not good at recognition or providing positive feedback. We also found that we did not celebrate small things. We were not recognizing our people as the most important resources and we were not training our work force to meet the challenges of the future."

Our executives analyzed Tennant's culture and environment by getting involved in small groups that cut across departmental lines. They learned to listen, and were trained in small group techniques. They took internal opinion surveys and published the results.

By showing an interest in what employees had to say, and by improving our skills, we were able to change our culture, behavior, and attitudes. Today we are better listeners and better managers. As a result, we have achieved *spontaneous small groups*. The achievement levels of the workers are higher, involvement is greater, costs are down, quality is up — and each person is important to the company.

Organizational Teamwork

By extensive use of vertical small groups, Tennant employees have developed a sense of product ownership. Such ownership provides a commitment to quality. But *horizontal* groups are also essential: functional areas should be closely integrated across the company's structure. Top department managers should cooperate in daily work and in new product development to "Do it right the first time."

Unlike many companies, Tennant has a vice president of manufacturing, engineering, and purchasing who assures that design engineering, manufacturing, quality and reliability engineering, materials control, and purchasing all work closely together.

Each department has its areas of responsibility, but works directly with the other departments. For example, purchasing and materials control are separate at Tennant. Purchasing decides which supplier to use and develops and maintains the supplier relationship. Materials control gets the day-by-day requirements and manages purchased material inventory; if problems arise, they work with one another as well as with other departments including engineering, manufacturing, and quality control. If necessary, purchasing will contact supplier top management to resolve problems.

New Product Development

We also take a team approach to developing new products and to enhancing existing products. Depending on the developmental phase, the team captain may be from any of several departments: engineering, purchasing, or a production depart-

> *This structure has worked well for us . . . reorganizing is not necessary to get results, though . . . the idea is to eliminate any barriers to working together for a common cause."*
> — Roger

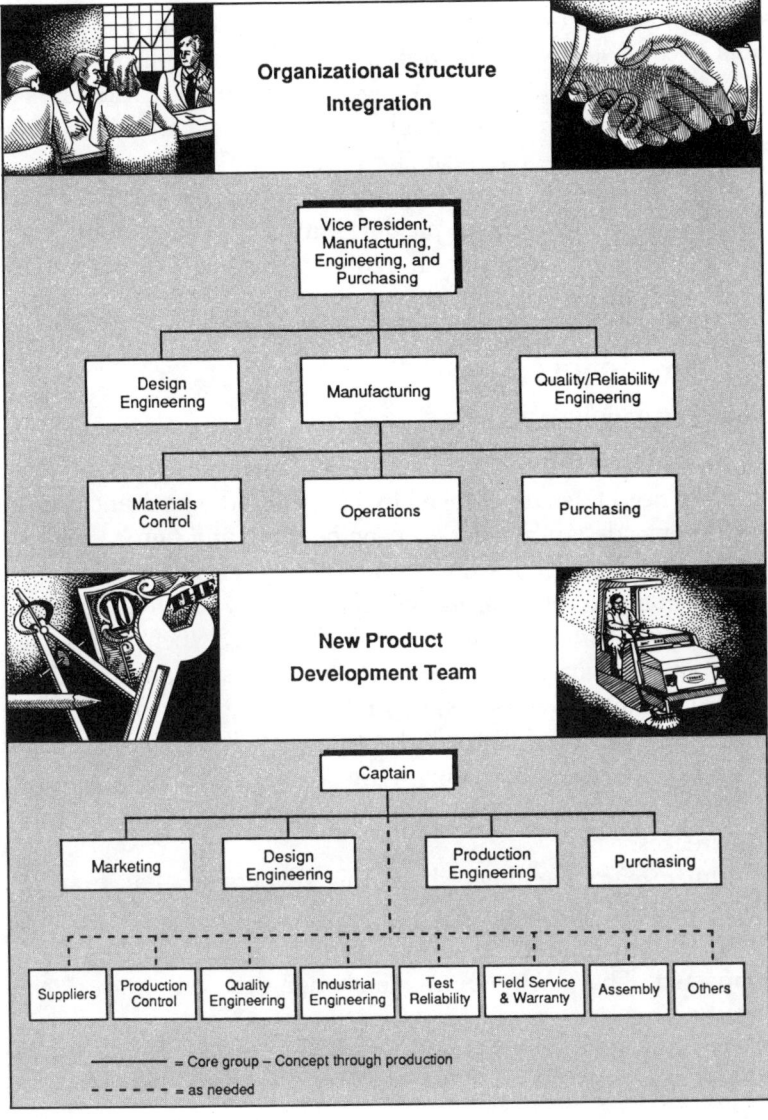

ment, for example. Team captains will change periodically. During the early idea search, a marketing person might be the captain. In the design phase, an engineer. Later, as we go into manufacturing, the captain might be from quality. In the audit phase, it might be a reliability engineer.

Product development teams have some ongoing members: marketing, design or production engineering, and purchasing. The dotted line on the previous chart indicates other areas that will be represented at the appropriate time: suppliers, production control, quality engineering, test reliability, field service, assembly, and others. Probably not permanent members, they are assigned as the team captain requests.

This concurrent engineering approach replaces the traditional approach of developing products in a series of steps each independent of the other. It reduces changes, rework, costs, and product development time.

Ownership for All Team Members

For a newly developed product to be a quality success, all team players need to share ownership, especially the permanent four: marketing, design, production engineering, and purchasing. All share responsibility for the product's long-term success.

For example, purchasing specialists can't wash their hands of the product after it goes into production. When component costs go up, purchasing must retain ownership and take costs out. Tennant provides detailed bill of materials reports, listing figures for both predicted and actual cost. If purchasing makes mistakes, or markets change, costs go up. Purchasing is on the team: they have to be accountable and work out the differences.

Other team members share this ownership. For example, engineering changes have a ripple-down effect on the product: cost, documentation, assembly, service and marketing are all impacted. That's why we make change decisions from a team perspective.

Team members find themselves wearing two hats — one for the corporation, another for their department. The corporate fedora covers their concern for the success of the whole product. The departmental hat is tailored to the team member's specialty. Purchasing might switch from the fedora to a green visor when going over the component procurement schedules. As Lynda Peterson, purchasing supervisor, says, "We work harder to select qualified suppliers in the first place because we know that the team is depending on us."

Melding Individual and Team Goals

Team members must share similar goals. Without teams, the quality manager might track only defects per machine. The assembly manager might focus only on schedules and efficiency, and engineering may care only about product performance. Unless people share similar goals, it's unlikely the goals will be met; it's as if people were following different maps and hoping to end up at the same place.

Our new product development teams decide on goals at their first meeting, using different criteria than in the past. For example, the design engineers ponder assembly's goals of manufacturability and assembly method. They know it's important to consider nut size and type of hose fitting to keep assembly simple: fewer wrenches speed assembly, so we try to use the same size nuts as often as possible; less diversity prevents mistakes, so we try to use identical parts whenever possible.

Teams can set goals to minimize engineering changes and then measure how well they do. When assembly and field service workers are on new product development teams, they can say, "We've tried that before and it didn't work" and be heard. It's an important statement early in the design phase.

Design, Development, and Documentation

As the design develops, purchasing starts sourcing — looking at qualified suppliers. With engineering, purchasing evaluates new technology, explores new sources, makes on-site visits, and contacts supplier top management. Two or three years before production, purchasing and Tennant management reach an understanding with the supplier's executives. That way, they aren't putting out fires at the last minute.

The next milestone is to verify documentation, including drawings and specifications. Everybody wants to be in the loop early in the documentation phase. In the past, quality control didn't see the drawings until they checked the piece; purchasing never saw them until they processed the requisition. Assembly didn't see the documentation until the parts were on the dock and waiting to be put together, or until they checked the drawing when parts didn't fit. All team members agree that users should check the documentation before the product is released to production.

When manufacturing starts up, the new production guidelines call for design, purchasing, manufacturing, production control, marketing, and others to test-drive the machines prior to the first production run.

A common strategy: build several quality-assurance models before going to market. Some team goals include:
- ▶ Reduced time to market
- ▶ Zero defect machines
- ▶ Productivity gains
- ▶ Meeting cost targets
- ▶ Reliability improvement

The team stays together over the next year or longer to monitor the goals, to get the product out, and ensure that it does what it's supposed to do.

Doing It Faster

Recently a Tennant group put together a new product development process. The group included representatives from design engineering, production engineering, quality control, purchasing, and manufacturing — all veterans of new product development teams.

Their goal was to "do it faster and better" to speed up the entire process and to release the product into manufacturing with fewer problems and less finger-pointing than is usual with

Telling Secrets

At Tennant, purchasing wanted to involve suppliers in the concurrent engineering approach to new product development. We began to invite groups of suppliers to full-day sessions where new product development was discussed.

In the morning sessions, suppliers were brought up to date on Tennant's quality, reliability, standardization, and cost-reduction goals. They were also given new product development information previously held secret.

In the afternoon, we held breakout groups. Supplier representatives were joined by a purchasing person and a design engineer. They discussed Tennant's needs in detail, with an eye to what the supplier could do to meet those needs while shortening development time.

We wanted to design our products with the latest technology and most cost-effective components. We also wanted to eliminate problems caused by misapplication of parts.

The results so far have exceeded our expectations. Suppliers have shared with us their new product development projects, allowing us to design with an eye to the future rather than the past.

We also found that suppliers leave these meetings with a much better understanding of our expectations, application requirements, and operating environments. They gain insight into what we want, and we gain insight into supplier capabilities so that we don't develop specifications that cannot be attained.

— Roger

new products.

Welders, sheet metal fabricators, assemblers, and of course suppliers all worked on the prototype team. The team captains, and everybody involved in the design, wanted their input. We've all bought into the idea of concurrent engineering: getting everybody's input is key.

The team came up with a formalized procedure flow, covering everything from the idea search to the final documentation check. Because every group in the company had input, some nonstandard criteria and early milestones were proposed.

For example, early in phase one, the idea development stage, team members called for a detailed development model, including profit, risk, specifications, costs, schedules, and market impact. Right away we started seeing ideas from engineering, model making, testing, purchasing, marketing, assembly, and quality. In the past, such input would have come much later in the process (and might have forced changes in plans already made).

The net result: this new product introduction set performance records in virtually every measurable category. It has become the model for other teams to follow and to beat.

Summary

Building a team attitude — giving all employees and suppliers ownership in the product — is a key goal in improving supplier quality. Teamwork means creating a cooperative attitude horizontally in the company, among various departments, and also vertically, among top management, middle management, and line employees. Everybody should know that he or she is important to the company. Every employee can make a contribution to a small group — for problem solving, planning, and otherwise assuring a quality product.

In this discussion, we've focused on Tennant's employee efforts as a guide to the types of programs we want to see in our suppliers' organizations.

There's no doubt our suppliers learn from our example. As Richard Sitarz said after his team from Prospect Foundry spent a day with our employees, "It is obvious that improving the quality of our operations will continue to pay dividends."

Chapter 5

Customer/Supplier Partnership

In the early 1980s, Roger visited our joint-venture partner in Japan. We were known for top-quality floor maintenance equipment and Roger was surprised to hear complaints from the Japanese about Tennant machines: hydraulic leaks were leaving oil spots on newly cleaned floors.

We'd heard few complaints about those machines in the United States, where we sold many more than in Japan. But there was no doubt: hydraulic leaks were a major concern for our Japanese customers. Upon investigating, we discovered that our American machines also leaked. American customers simply figured this was normal; the Japanese didn't.

The Hydraulic Leak Affair

We formed a small group of employees to identify the source of the hydraulic leaks and tackle the problem. The team captain was from top management. As we studied the leaks, we made some interesting discoveries:

- ▶ *Suppliers* — Tennant was using 16 different suppliers for hydraulic hoses and fittings. Most of the time we simply ordered from a distributor; we didn't know the manufacturers, and they didn't know us. We immediately cut back to two suppliers. Now we have only one supplier for hoses and fittings.
- ▶ *Design* — The machine's designers often didn't consider the number of joints to assemble or allow enough room inside the machine to do the assembly work. Turning the wrenches, holding the hoses, adjusting the fittings — all were difficult and inefficient procedures. Now, assemblers and suppliers get involved in the design stage to make sure the joints are designed for ease of assembly.
- ▶ *Training* — To fix a leak, conventional wisdom was to tighten the fitting. Ironically, too-tight fittings were a major cause of leaks. We reduced our supplier base, and we trained our people, with supplier assistance, in proper hose installation. Since then, we've dramatically reduced leaks.

All of these discoveries reinforced the need for teamwork.

By involving purchasing, the supplier, the assemblers, design engineering, the field staff, and others, we learned critical information. More importantly, we were able to apply what we learned — and improve our product quality.

In 1980, we were counting leaks per hundred joints; by 1985 we had less than one leak per thousand joints. With continued work, we're now way beyond our previous measures. We now count leaks per ten-thousand joints.

We learned many important lessons from what we term "the hydraulic leak affair." The biggest lesson: to be successful in quality improvement, partnerships must be formed and maintained with suppliers. Thus, the third critical success factor in improving supplier quality is developing *customer/supplier partnerships*.

The successful partnership is different in every situation, but it always works to the benefit of both parties and strengthens over the long term.

For example, Trojan Battery in Santa Fe Springs, California, supplies batteries to Tennant. Rick Godber, president, says Trojan is happy to accept our quality standards. "Tennant is our favorite account," he says. "Most purchasers are overly conscious of price. Tennant certainly cares about price, but quality is on top. That's our philosophy, too. It's not just price — it's delivering a quality product on time. What Tennant is doing is good for us, it's good for them, it's good for the whole American economy."

Rick's especially impressed that we nurture the customer/supplier relationship once it's developed. "Tennant comes here every year. They stimulate everyone in our organization to do their best. When the customer cares so much, you care more."

Dorothy Keifer, our material controller who handles the day-to-day relationship with Trojan, says the relationship is so good that Trojan is supplying batteries on a weekly, just-in-time basis, shipping cross-country from California. "We FAX them the order, they ship on Friday, and their trucks are here on Tuesday," she says, noting that Tennant's previous battery supplier "was physically closer to us, but they weren't as cooperative. Distance isn't an issue when you deal with quality people."

Lynda Peterson, Tennant's purchasing supervisor in charge of the Trojan account, says Trojan became Tennant's first just-in-time supplier after the previous large manufacturer supplying batteries "just couldn't understand what we needed." Trojan is different. "They want to work with us. Whatever our needs, they want to respond. They understand what it takes to stay in business."

Tennant is not Trojan's partner in terms of legal ownership. We focus on our own business — floor maintenance. However, we are Trojan's partners in commerce — working together to succeed in business. Our relationship is akin to the Japanese "keiretsu" business consortia, in which companies align together based on trust and loyalty, working in each other's interest against other market forces.

What Makes the Partnership Work?

The Trojan story highlights several important qualities of the customer/supplier relationship:
- ▶ Communication
- ▶ Sharing zero defects philosophy
- ▶ Mutual trust
- ▶ Close working relationships at all levels
- ▶ Knowledge of customer applications
- ▶ Capable and willing to work together to solve problems

Ideally you want to work with your suppliers on a permanent basis to achieve the same end: success in business. Of course, the world is not ideal and change is inevitable, so your partnership may not last forever, and one party may benefit more than the other. Still, your goals should be clear.

Communication

We can't overemphasize the importance of communication. Keep the lines open — communicate often. If it makes sense to go visit a supplier, then go visit. Walk through their plant and talk to people, or invite them to your plant. Establish relationships and have your people get to know their people. That is absolutely crucial.

Proactive Communication. We create several opportunities for communication. We meet with top supplier management very early in the relationship. We try to communicate as many of our needs as possible during this conference. We attempt to understand their needs. We get to know them, and we nurture the relationship.

Another proactive opportunity is training. We offer training for suppliers in a series of conferences, seminars, and other types of meetings. We send our engineers out to help suppliers in their plants. We teach them how to use our reports and how to improve quality-control processes. Training allows us to work more closely with suppliers. Also, it's often a help to small companies. One of our Wisconsin suppliers has sent dozens of people to Minneapolis for training; the company is too small to have a training staff and they like the training we provide.

Reactive Communication. Reactive opportunities occur when suppliers come to us with questions, problems, or sometimes complaints, and we answer. In these situations, we can build relationships in very positive ways, especially when giving out information or solving problems. Failure data analysis and reporting is another opportunity for reactive communication. We react to the supplier's parts failures, and when they get our report, they are expected to react as well. We defuse these situations by emphasizing the positive — but without minimizing our expectations.

Sharing Zero Defects Philosophy

We look for a shared understanding of how zero defects benefits both customer and supplier. Suppliers must be willing to commit to a focus of providing total customer satisfaction. The zero defects philosophy simply means that things can and must be better. Suppliers must share this vision and constantly challenge themselves to make continuous improvement.

Mutual Trust

Partnerships can only be based on mutual trust. Mutual trust leads to open and candid communication. Do suppliers inform you when you're causing them problems? Do they accept responsibility for problems they cause? Do they disclose their long-term research and production plans? Do they respect the confidential information you disclose?

Another element in mutual trust is some assurance of long-term commitment. You want to depend on your partners being there when you need them. They want to do the same. Long-term commitment is based partly on history and experience, partly on communication, and partly on each partner's good faith in the enterprise.

Evidence of mutual trust is seen when both parties share new product development from an early stage and in an ongoing manner. At Tennant we have found that involving our suppliers at the design stage has improved our products. Since they are the experts in their fields, they prevent us from making mistakes, help us save money and time, and help us "Do it right the first time."

Keeping our partners involved has given us quality control and testing resources far beyond our own capacity. We have been able to incorporate new technology and proprietary ideas. We have gained the benefit of countless brilliant researchers working in our partners' labs.

Close Working Relationships at All Levels

We look for the opportunity to develop close working relationships at all levels. We encourage one-on-one contacts. Our quality people talk to their quality people. Our design engineers meet their design engineers. Our marketers might learn some important features and benefits from their marketers — and they might learn some success stories about their products from our marketing reps. After all, they are both moving the same product.

We have benefited from close working relationships in big

ways. We can send some of our suppliers a new Tennant machine, ask them to improve it, and get excellent results. As we use supplier components, whether hoses, motors, or widgets, we provide feedback which helps them improve. Over the years, our engineers have rearranged some supplier production lines, provided quality training, and worked on reducing setup time in production, among other things.

Knowledge of Customer Applications

We look for supplier knowledge of our business and applications. If their technical experts study our products and gain some insight into our applications, they can apply their experience and training to our concerns. On the other hand, if they don't know our company or our product lines, we don't believe they can add any value to our products. By working closely with suppliers during new product development, by sharing operating conditions and environments, and by clearly defining reliability goals, we ensure that the right components are selected for the application.

Working Together to Solve Problems

Developing a win/win relationship between supplier and manufacturer requires mutual trust and a commitment to working toward each other's success. When a problem occurs, rather than finger-pointing, the emphasis is on working together to identify the problem and then to develop a permanent solution. The ultimate goal is to have processes in place that prevent problems from happening in the first place.

Preventing problems is so critical that we've devoted a separate chapter to it, but let's look briefly at the two elements of problem solving: identifying problems and establishing permanent solutions.

Identifying Problems

In many cases, the hardest part of solving problems is properly identifying the problems that exist: What are they? How extensive are they? People have to care enough to report problems. The corporate climate has to encourage problem identification.

Some of our people remember when assemblers would come up with make-do solutions on the line, rather than contacting an engineer or supervisor who really didn't want to get involved. If there's no reward in identifying problems, if no one gives you credit when you report something wrong, then who's going to do it? Management has to create a climate that says, "Don't hide anything. We want to know what's going on. We need your help. We can't do it without you."

Ten years into it, we've found that identifying problems is part of Tennant's culture. Our people know that it's good to report problems and deal with them immediately. We want them to report an oil drop on a newly polished floor.

In changing our culture, we worked with those who could tackle the problem. We encouraged engineers to go out on the assembly line and take notes. In the old culture at Tennant, engineers were focused on design. Communicating with the line wasn't a big priority.

Workers get disgusted and discouraged when no one does anything to solve the problems they bring up. They decide it's not worth the effort to identify problems. They adopt the "bigger hammer approach" — since it doesn't help to talk to engineering, just get a bigger hammer and whack it a good one.

You want a company climate where it's worthwhile to identify problems. Give all employees a voice. Train top management, managers, supervisors, professional staff to listen. With the proper attitude and encouragement, people will get together informally to identify and solve problems.

Formal approaches also help. Over the past few years, we've developed several tools for identifying problems. Each is useful as we develop win/win partnerships with our suppliers:

- ► Nonconformance reporting
- ► Error cause identification system
- ► Pareto analysis

> *Purchased parts cause us significantly fewer problems in assembly today than they did in the past. Our internal efforts, as well as those of our suppliers, continue to pay dividends. While we're pleased with our progress to date, we must challenge ourselves and our suppliers to continue improvements in the future."*
> — Don

Tennant Rework Hours — Purchased Parts
(AS A PERCENT OF ASSEMBLY ACTIVITY)

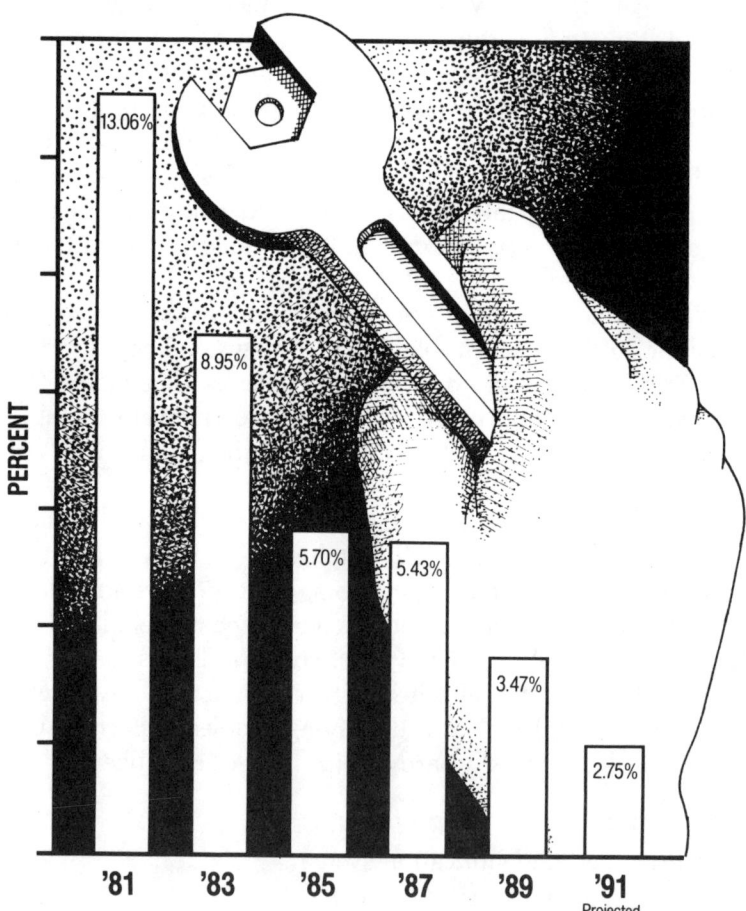

Year	Percent
'81	13.06%
'83	8.95%
'85	5.70%
'87	5.43%
'89	3.47%
'91 Projected	2.75%

Nonconformance Reporting. One of our formal problem-solving methods is our nonconformance report (NCR), a form on which we report all nonconforming parts.

When doing the nonconformance report, we first identify where the defective part came from. Was it found in incoming inspection? During final assembly? In our stock?

First we list the quantity inspected versus rejected, and we describe the defects. Next the department to be charged for the defect is indicated, such as paint, warehouse, welding, or assembly. Purchasing may be charged if the problem is supplier caused. Maybe engineering is charged, since they wrote the specs. Finally, the disposition is noted. It might include scrapping the part, reworking it, or returning it to the supplier.

The point is, all of these outcomes are measures of defective parts. With this information, we are able to quickly and effectively identify and solve the problems.

Error Cause Identification System. Our error cause identification (ECI) system is another formal process we've developed to solve both internal and supplier problems which have evaded informal solutions. The idea: make someone at Tennant specifically accountable. The ECI is a form readily available to all employees, and individuals simply state the problem. Those causing the problem are then held responsible for solving it. If the problem is bigger than one person can handle, we bring a group together. When the ECI initiator agrees that the problem has been solved, the case is closed.

When we began this program, we received hundreds of ECIs. In fact, within the first six months we'd received so many that we put a moratorium on the process and declared Super Saturdays when employees came in to work through the backlog.

We still have the ECI program, but it's no longer getting the use it once did. People don't feel they have to write notes to make problems known; they can make a phone call instead. With the help of the ECI, we changed our corporate culture to be more open to identifying problems.

When working with suppliers, the secret is to begin with a formal system. Work through the forms, identify the problems,

> *The NCR is an important problem notification device on purchased parts. Procurement specialists in purchasing give top priority to resolving the problems, often working closely with the supplier. These reports are input to our suppliers' performance data base."*
> — Tim

TENNANT — NONCONFORMANCE REPORT

Q.C. USE ONLY	SOURCE:	Qty.	Part #
Defective Part # _____	[1] Inspection (Order # _____)	Date / /	Description
Defective Qty. _____	[2] Internal Dept. (Last Op # _____)		
Defect Code _____	[3] Other Dept. _____	Dept. #	Originator
Description Code _____	[4] Final Assy. (Machine Model # _____)		
Supplier Code _____	(Engine Serial # _____)	Rev. #	Inspected By:
Supplier:	[5] Stock		

CHARGE EXPENSE TO: (Circle One Only)

[02] Paint	[10] Shp./Crtg. I	[18] Ind. Eng.	[66] Marketing	[A1] Sheetmetal	[B0] Shipping II
[03] Assy. I	[11] Stkrm./Rec. I	[20] Prod. Imp.	[67] Int'l	[A4] Mach. Shop	[B1] Whse./Rec. II
[05] Welding	[13] S.F.C.	[21] Prod. Eng.	[68] Legal	[A8] Brush	[B2] T-Die
[06] Zane Whse.	[14] T-Crib I	[22] Matl. Control	[88] Purchasing	[A9] Q.C. II	[B4] T-Crib II
[07] Assy. II	[16] Maint. I	[62] Warranty	[96] Engineering		[B6] Maint. II
[09] Q.C. I	[17] Prod. Cont.	[65] Traffic	[99] Multiple Dept. List: _____		Sign Off:

Qty. Inspected	Qty. Rejected	Description of Defects

Sign Off: Q.C.	Disposition Date	DISPOSITION: (Circle One Only)
Other	/ /	[1] Use As Is [3] Rework [5] RTV-Credit [7] RTV-Rework
		[2] Scrap [4] Split [6] RTV-Replacement (P. O. # _____)

W.C. #	Operation #	Operation	Qty.	Sign-Off Complete

CORRECTIVE ACTION   #

PART # TO BE SCRAPPED				STOCK AS PART #				
Qty. Pulled	Pulled By	Pull Date	Scrap Qty.	Scrapped By	Stk. Loc.	Qty. Rec'd.	Rec'd. By	Rec'd. Date

and make things happen. Let the employees see change. People will be going out of their way to help. We have one supplier who's in our plant so much, helping with new ideas, that he has a Tennant employee ID badge!

First it's necessary to build trust and establish a problem-solving atmosphere. Major change takes time. The ECI gives all Tennant employees an indirect link to our suppliers. As problems get solved, the supplier/customer relationship gets stronger and stronger.

Pareto Analysis. Pareto analysis is a way to categorize problems so that you can work on the biggest ones first. We've found the use of Pareto analysis to be a powerful way to communicate with suppliers. By collecting and displaying data, we can graphically summarize problems and suppliers can see what they must do to improve their quality. As we've all heard so often, "A picture's worth a thousand words." Most suppliers are eager to please: if you can help them see the problem, they'll do their best to solve it.

That's what Tennant found when we approached our wire harness supplier, Monona Wire, about improving delivery. Although they went to heroic efforts to make sure we never had to shut down our line — every week we were worried. Sometimes we even sent drivers out to meet the Monona delivery truck as it came up Interstate 35 from Iowa. Delivery needed to get better.

Finally, Materials Control Supervisor Patrick Hargarten, Procurement Specialist Rich Carlson, and others worked with Monona people on ways to improve. As it turned out, Monona's executives hadn't realized how important on-time delivery was to us. They were more focused on product quality. Once they got the message, things changed and they quickly began making 100 percent of their deliveries on time. They've maintained that 100 percent ever since without sacrificing product quality.

Establishing Permanent Solutions

Once we identify a problem, whether from customer reports or through tools used in production, such as the NCR or Pareto analysis, we take steps to solve it. We take whatever immediate

> *We use the Pareto analysis technique to identify and quantify our biggest problems. They are categorized by all combined commodities, by individual commodities, by supplier, and other ways. This allows us to concentrate our resources effectively.*
> — Don

Sample Pareto Analysis of Problems
(PURCHASED PARTS)

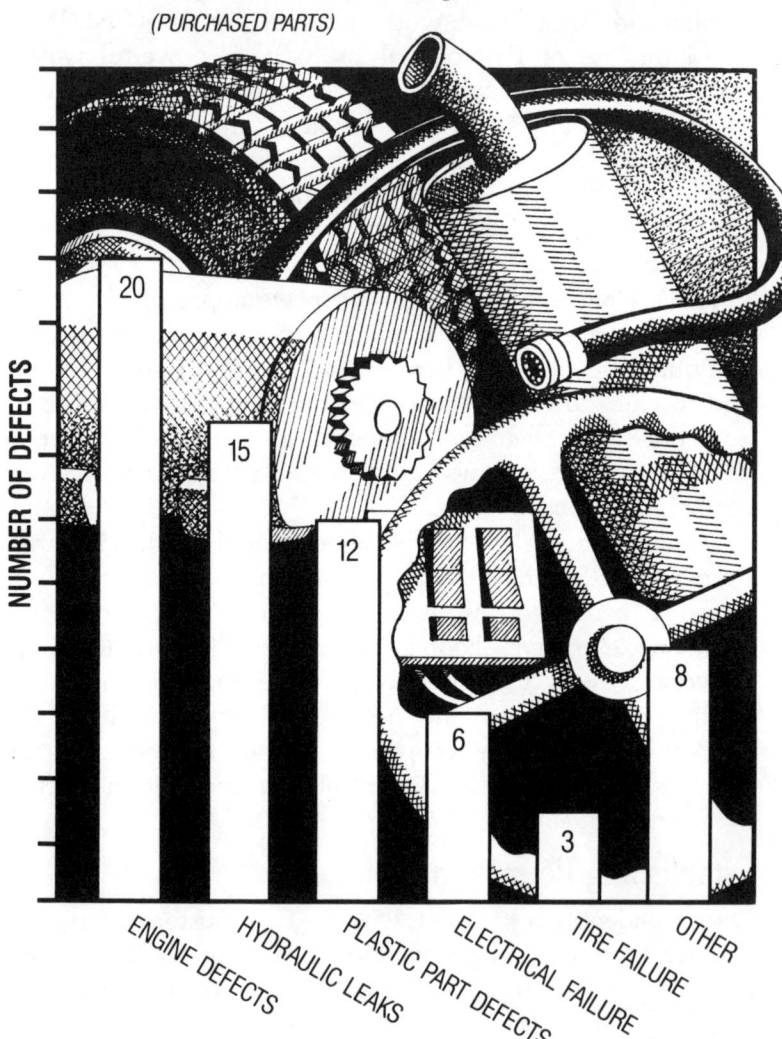

action is necessary and then work to establish a permanent solution to the problem. We go to the source: we change our procedures or ask the supplier to change theirs.

Supplier Corrective Action Request. A formal problem-solving method involves a form developed by quality engineering: the supplier corrective action request (SCAR). We use these forms when we find rejected parts in incoming inspection or final machine assembly and test. The form:

▶ Notifies suppliers of nonconformance
▶ Documents corrective action
▶ Ensures permanent solution

At Tennant, we ask for a supplier response within two weeks, including a reason for the discrepancy and a statement of corrective action. We expect meaningful, on-time answers, 100 percent of the time.

Our quality engineering group reads and rates each response. We want evidence that the supplier understands what caused the problem. "Operator error," for example, is not an acceptable explanation.

The goal is process change. For example, we don't want a supplier to simply send a free replacement when a product is bad. We want an end to the underlying problem. Suppliers should tell us what process change took place and how they are doing it differently now. *Training* is an acceptable response, as is a *change in material or process,* or even a change in the original specification to establish a *new spec.*

When evaluating our suppliers' responses to corrective action requests, we look at the promptness and acceptability of the response. If the response is late, we want to know why. When we visit the supplier, we monitor how they're implementing the changes they promised: are they doing what they said they would do?

When we first began this program, we issued many supplier corrective action requests — one every time a part was rejected. Now that our suppliers know the program and our standards, we issue fewer requests. Sometimes, rather than issuing a request, we communicate informally and still get the desired results.

> *" We think this is an excellent example of a solid customer/supplier relationship."*
> — Roger

Good Supplier Relationship Reaps Mutual Rewards

Monona Wire, a small company in Monona, Iowa, used to be on our blacklist. The wire harnesses they supplied for Tennant machines were sometimes defective and often they would not make shipment dates or ship complete orders.

That was how we started our relationship with Monona about 10 years ago. For a while, everybody at Tennant wanted to find someone else — Monona Wire had a bad name. At that time, Tennant had five or six suppliers of wire harnesses and no formal program with suppliers. But because of the problems we were experiencing with Monona as well as other suppliers, we decided to work more closely with them to improve the relationship.

This happened at a time when Tennant recognized that our problems with suppliers were mostly our own. We started to see the value in working with a supplier rather than going to someone new with a whole new set of problems. Purchasing initiated a project with our Engineering Department and Monona Wire to develop standards for parts drawings in an effort to improve the quality of parts. This was also a crucial time for Monona Wire, as a new person — Loren Smith — had just become president of their operations. He became our principal contact there.

Loren was the turning point. He was a dynamic leader. Under Smith, things got better. He came to Tennant's supplier ZD Day in 1985 and became interested in what we were doing and saying about quality. As our relationship with Monona Wire improved, so did the quality of parts. However, there were still areas of the relationship that needed improving — shipments were still delayed.

Tennant again visited Loren and stressed how important on-time deliveries and full shipments were. Monona began to take our messages seriously. In 1987 they improved their on-time deliveries from 60% to 95%. In 1988 and 1989 their shipments were 100% on time. Partial shipments were down to zero.

Parts defects had also improved. In 1989 we used 28,300 Monona parts and only 23 were rejected — an extraordinary turnaround! Monona Wire had gone from the blacklist to a real success. Today they are our sole supplier for wire harnesses.

In 1989 Monona Wire received "Special Recognition" for their outstanding performance. Being nominated to receive this recognition requires more than just meeting our quality and delivery goals. Monona excels in all aspects of our business relationship. They had to demonstrate that they were going over and above the standard.

Their efforts to improve the business relationship haven't stopped. They continually look for ways to make it even more beneficial. Patrick Hargarten, Tennant material control supervisor, can attest to how much easier Monona has made the receiving process.

"I used to spend an hour and a half a day figuring out the shipments from Monona — they were a paperwork and expediting nightmare. Now I spend more like 15 minutes a week on the same task," he says. Monona also continues to work with our Engineering Department offering suggestions for improving parts design. Their quality outlook and desire to maintain good business relations have earned them new respect at Tennant.

Once you've identified the problem, the supplier will usually take steps to solve it. The key to getting a *permanent* solution, in most cases, is to establish and communicate your expectations. Our goals are communicated to our suppliers. They're crystal clear, as you'll note from the chart about Supplier Quality Goals.

Summary

To achieve the greatest success in quality improvement, we're convinced that partnerships must be formed with suppliers and meticulously nurtured. The partnership should include common goals and a win/win attitude for both parties.

Different situations result in different types of partnerships. But, as we pointed out in this chapter, all partnerships have some common characteristics:

- ▶ *Communication.* Enhance communication and strengthen the customer/supplier partnership through the use of small groups and a variety of problem-solving techniques.
- ▶ *Shared Zero Defect Philosophy.* Establish a shared zero defect philosophy to help strengthen common goals that are mutually beneficial.
- ▶ *Mutual Trust.* Be able to count on the partner. This strengthens the open and candid communication that is critical to a successful partnership.
- ▶ *Close Working Relationships.* Involve all levels of management and other personnel in close working relationships. One person alone can't develop and maintain an ongoing, interactive relationship. It takes a team effort.
- ▶ *Knowledge of Customer Applications.* Learn about the customer's business. The better we understand each other's applications, the better the quality results will be.
- ▶ *Working Together to Solve Problems.* Be proactive. The ultimate goal of the partnership is to have a process in place that will prevent problems from happening.

Recognizing suppliers as partners has proven to be a very successful approach for us. In fact, it's probably our most effective and important tool for improving quality.

> *If we have a problem with a supplier part, we identify what the problem is and why it's a problem for us. The supplier must tell us what corrective action they are putting in place to prevent a recurrence. We expect and often receive immediate response from our suppliers."*
> — Ron

TENNANT	**SUPPLIER CORRECTIVE ACTION REQUEST**	NO. _____

SUPPLIER:	TENNANT P/N	REF. NSR	DATE
	SUPPLIER P/N	REQUEST ORIGINATOR	
	PART NAME	PROCUREMENT SPECIALIST	

REJECT FOUND IN:
☐ INCOMING INSPC. P.O. # _____ QUANTITY _____ NO. INSPECTED _____ NO. REJECTED _____ % REJECTED _____
☐ FINAL MACHINE TEST NO. REJECTED _____ BETWEEN _____ MONTHLY USAGE _____ % REJECTED _____

REQUIREMENT AND NON-CONFORMITY

DISPOSITION OF PARTS
☐ USE AS IS ☐ REWORKED AT TENNANT ☐ RETURNED ON P.O. # _____ ☐ SCRAP AT TENNANT

☐ THIS CORRECTIVE ACTION REQUEST IS FOR THE SUPPLIER'S INFORMATION ONLY.
☐ THIS CORRECTIVE ACTION REQUEST IS DIRECTED TO THE SUPPLIER FOR INVESTIGATION AND STATEMENT OF CORRECTIVE ACTION. THIS REQUEST MUST BE ANSWERED COMPLETELY AND ACCURATELY BEFORE _____ .

REASON FOR DISCREPANCY:

STATEMENT OF CORRECTIVE ACTION (ATTACH ADDITIONAL INFORMATION AS REQUIRED)

EFFECTIVITY DATE:	INVESTIGATOR:	DEPARTMENT:	DATE

DISTRIBUTION:
 White & Green - Return to Originator when completed
 Yellow - Retain for use by Investigating and Answering Dept.
 Pink - Retain as Originator's Copy (for follow-up)
 Gold - Retain in Purchasing (for follow-up)

RETURN PARTS 1 & 2 TO:
 Tennant Company
 701 No. Lilac Drive
 P.O. Box 1452
 Minneapolis, MN 55440
 ATTN: Q.C. Department

Supplier Quality Goals

▶ *Tennant and its suppliers will work together in full cooperation and harmony, and with mutual respect.*

▶ *Suppliers have the responsibility to deliver exactly the product and/or service they have promised.*

▶ *Tennant's established performance goals in the areas of quality, reliability, and delivery must be met by all suppliers.*

▶ *Suppliers must take full ownership for the products and services they provide. When problems exist, they must act with a strong sense of urgency in working with Tennant to resolve the problem and to permanently correct the process that caused it.*

▶ *Tennant's vision that things can and must be better must be shared by all suppliers and they must constantly challenge themselves to make continuous improvement.*

▶ *Suppliers must commit to Tennant's quality focus of fulfilling the needs of our customers and providing total customer satisfaction.*

Chapter 6

Preventing Problems from Reaching the Customer

otorola, Inc., a winner of the Malcolm Baldrige National Quality Award in 1988, is one example of an American company that is determined to keep problems from reaching the customer. Motorola's managers literally carry a card with them stating their corporate goal of "total customer satisfaction."

Faced with the rapid rise of Japanese electronics firms in the world market, Motorola began an almost evangelical crusade to improve quality. Managers wear beepers so they're available to customers; they regularly visit customer businesses. As a result, most Motorola products have increased their market share, here and abroad.

As Motorola and other companies have found, long-term success invariably requires that you prevent problems from reaching the customer. That is, surveys show you'll never hear about half your failures. Of the failures you do hear about, no matter what extra steps you take to satisfy the customer, you'll regain only about half the business. The tragedy: for every 100 product failures, you'll lose 75 customers forever.

For all these reasons, *problem prevention* is the fourth critical success factor in our list of ways to enhance supplier quality. Help your suppliers prevent problems from reaching you, their customer, and you'll have an easier time preventing problems from reaching your customers.

We routinely survey Tennant customers to learn what matters to them. They consistently list four major purchase criteria:

- ▶ Performance — functions as promised
- ▶ Reliability — continues to perform over time
- ▶ Durability — withstands wear and tear
- ▶ Serviceability — easy to maintain

To keep problems from reaching our customers, we pay close attention to these four areas. We look for performance, reliability, durability, and serviceability in the products we purchase from our suppliers and in the products we manufacture.

Tools for Problem Prevention

Our top-down emphasis on quality, team approach to new product development, building of Tennant/supplier partnerships, measuring and reporting on quality, supplier qualification process, and our annual business management sessions have all helped us prevent problems with purchased parts. We also have found three technical tools to be useful in preventing problems:

1. *Specification development and review* — a process that ensures that specifications are developed to meet everyone's needs. Throughout the design process, our design engineering group establishes component specifications and provides drawings to purchasing, quality engineering, and our suppliers for their review and input. During the last phase of design, we do a thorough inspection and testing of all prototype and sample parts to ensure that the specified part will do the job.
2. *Statistical process control* — a measurement and evaluation tool that helps Tennant and suppliers make sure that all parts are consistently produced according to specifications.
3. *Reliability emphasis* — a measurement and evaluation tool that helps determine and predict component and system reliability. We measure quality over time and identify areas for design improvement.

Let's look at the application and use of each of these problem-prevention tools.

Specification Development and Review (SDR)

We begin by bringing departments together to jointly develop specifications before finalizing drawings and releasing a product to production. Our goals are to:

- ▶ Increase the design engineer's awareness and consideration of internal and external customer needs.
- ▶ Ensure that all new engineering specifications are accurate and understood internally and by suppliers.

▶ Prevent engineering changes after products are released for manufacturing.

It took us some time to get used to working together on specification development and review. When we first began this process, design engineers asked purchasing people: "Who are you to review my drawing?" To quality engineers, who needed a criteria for evaluating a part, design engineers said "Don't worry, it'll be there." We had to carefully present and explain the reasons for change, but once they were understood, everybody bought in.

Purchasing obviously has a legitimate need to be involved in developing the drawing. The specifications often determine whether or not preferred suppliers can be used, or even if the part can be purchased consistently to print. Senior Procurement Specialist Rick Anderson believes, "This is a key time to look for major quality and reliability improvements, cost reductions, and standardization opportunities. Supplier input is important, too. After all, suppliers are the ones ultimately responsible for conforming to the specifications."

Quality control also has good reasons to evaluate the drawings. In order to evaluate incoming parts they need information from the drawings — correct specs, measurable features. The supplier is in trouble and so is Tennant if information is missing, or incorrect, or if the tolerances are beyond the process capability. Quality control also has a wealth of information based on past experiences with similar parts, which comes in very handy during this stage of specification development.

Ask Questions on the Drawing. When purchasing and quality engineering review a drawing, they ask questions of the design engineer right on the drawing. For example, purchasing is concerned with the potential supplier. The designer may note a *specified* manufacturer, meaning they want to buy from a particular source. Or they may note a *reference* manufacturer, meaning the part may be made by many different companies, and purchasing can decide where to get it. If they specify *no* manufacturer, purchasing is supposed to find a source.

Purchasing will always raise questions about a specified

manufacturer. If Tennant is not currently doing business with that supplier or had trouble with them in the past, purchasing will certainly discuss alternatives with the design engineer. If the specified manufacturer is finally accepted, following an in-depth supplier assessment, their part number is put right on the drawing, making the spec as clear as possible.

Quality control has different concerns. For example, we recently considered a die-cut rubber part, with overall dimensions toleranced at +/− 30 thousandths. Quality control asked the designer if such tight tolerance was needed, or if it had been noted arbitrarily. From past experience, quality control knew that such a tolerance level is a problem and may cost extra time and money in manufacturing.

At the same meeting, purchasing asked about the material specification. Several different grades of rubber, all with different performance characteristics, were available that would meet the requirements on the drawing. Purchasing also mentioned that service people might have a hard time keeping these parts separate from similar parts. Embossing identification numbers on the parts solves that problem. Following a discussion with the supplier, that spec was added to the drawing.

Design engineering's final drawing included some changes. For example, tolerances were changed to +/- 60 thousandths; the material spec was clarified; and the Tennant part numbers will be embossed. We now have a much better specification, thanks to engineering, as well as purchasing, quality control, and the supplier.

Other Benefits of SDR. The specification development and review process has made other contributions to "Doing it right the first time." For example:

▶ We discovered we had been specifying and buying the same part under multiple part numbers. Through the review process, we standardized hoses, fittings, and other parts.

▶ We established generic prints. After standardizing parts, we standardized formats. Now the supplier gets all specs in one format.

▶ We're processing fewer and fewer engineering changes caused by failures. Obviously, we still make some changes due to performance or design alterations, but not because we've failed to do it right the first time.

Statistical Process Control Methods (SPC)

Statistical Process Control involves measuring and testing parts and collecting data to help us and our suppliers better control the manufacturing process. SPC is a fast-growing and powerful tool being used by today's world-class manufacturers.

Companies that interpret and use SPC will have an important competitive edge. That's why we give employees SPC training. Purchasing professionals, quality control inspectors, engineers, managers at all levels, and people on the production line need to understand and be able to interpret SPC data.

A few definitions will help you understand SPC basics and how SPC can help you and your suppliers:

▶ *Statistics* is the branch of math that lets you draw conclusions about the whole population from a data sample. It includes rules for collecting, organizing, and interpreting the numbers.

▶ *Process* refers to all the people and operations involved in manufacturing products, including design, purchasing, fabrication, assembly, testing, inspection, and the equipment involved.

▶ *Control* means keeping the manufacturing process within set bounds.

When reviewing SPC measurements, it's important to identify the:

▶ *Mean*, or average

▶ *Range* — distance between the highest and lowest measure

▶ *Standard deviation*, or amount of variation in the data

Senior Procurement Specialist Cynthia Fuller was one of the first persons in Tennant's purchasing department to receive SPC training. She uses it regularly for her commodities, and

> "We're not experts in the use of SPC, but we recognize that it's a powerful tool in helping prevent problems. In our sourcing decisions, we want to know if the supplier's process is capable of producing our parts consistently to print and whether or not the process is in control. It should be routine procedure for those responsible for making the part and for those who purchase it to be able to interpret capability reports and make decisions accordingly."
> — Tim

TENNANT CAPABILITY REPORT

Part # _Sample_   Dim. being measured _0.370 ± 0.010_

PART READINGS:

1: .379	11: .380	21: .373	31:	41:
2: .378	12: .377	22: .378	32:	42:
3: .376	13: .377	23: .375	33:	43:
4: .378	14: .378	24: .374	34:	44:
5: .381	15: .379	25: .378	35:	45:
6: .379	16: .378	26: .376	36:	46:
7: .378	17: .375	27: .377	37:	47:
8: .374	18: .380	28: .380	38:	48:
9: .379	19: .377	29: .376	39:	49:
10: .381	20: .377	30: .375	40:	50:

Changes A _____ D _____
         B _____ E _____
         C _____ F _____

Highest Reading _0.381_   Lowest Reading _0.373_   Range _0.008_
USL _0.380_   LSL _0.360_   Total Tolerance _0.020_
Mean (x̄) _0.377_   Standard Deviation (s) _0.002_
3s _0.006_   6s _0.012_
x̄ + 3s _0.383_   x̄ - 3s _0.371_
CP _1.63_   CPK _0.42_

she says: "Just as no two snowflakes or fingerprints are alike, no two parts are exactly alike. Variation is a given. Once this is accepted, and SPC tools are used, decisions can be made to modify the process or specifications based on data. Guesswork is eliminated. SPC data enables all parties to speak the same language."

SPC at Tennant. Before Tennant's quality emphasis, we generally measured just one or two pieces, even though that practice violated the laws of statistics which state how many pieces must be measured for a valid estimate. We assumed that our suppliers had quality controls in place which assured all future parts would be like initial samples. We disregarded the possibility of process variation.

Today, we use SPC to do process capability studies. At Tennant, we use 30 parts minimum, and we fill out a capability report. We look for suppliers who understand and use SPC tools; we provide training to those who don't. Sometimes we find suppliers who use SPC only upon request. In such cases, our quality engineers work with the suppliers to develop inspection plans, including the SPC tools we want used.

Reliability Emphasis

Reliability emphasis is another problem prevention tool we use at Tennant. We define reliability as "the probability a product will conform to its specifications throughout its expected life." Another way to put it is *quality over time.* The machine meets its specifications when we deliver it, as well as six months later, 12 months later, and so on.

Reliability is a statistical measure. The technical definition is: *the probability that a product will perform without failure for a specified period of time under specified operating conditions.* Mathematically we can determine reliability for a product's useful life.

When we figure reliability, we first gather data about product failures, operating time, and mission time. A *product failure* refers to any component that must be repaired or replaced. *Operating time* is figured in hours — the number of hours that the machine is running. *Mission time* for us is usually one year.

As with SPC, there are many reliability tools. Some help the test engineer predict product or system reliability during the testing phase and recommend changes if necessary. Another tool we've found useful breaks down a product's reliability by system and individual component. With this tool, the *block diagram*, we've been able to prevent problems on new products.

Reliability Committee. In 1983 we formed a reliability committee to establish a way to measure and improve our product reliability. It's been active ever since. This committee collects and analyzes data on failures, works with suppliers, tests reliability processes, and conducts reliability training.

Including members of engineering, quality control, marketing, warranty, manufacturing, and purchasing, the committee began by measuring warranty failures. They then identified a top-20 hit list of failures by part numbers and took action. By identifying and working on the less reliable parts, substantial results are being achieved, making Tennant machines more reliable year after year.

And the payoff goes to our customers — the true beneficiaries of all our efforts. We've extended product warranties, boosting them from 12 months on parts and 30 days on labor to 24 months on parts and six months on labor. Plus, Tennant's "Ultimate Performance Guarantee" allows customers to return a new machine for a full refund anytime during the first six months of ownership if not completely satisfied.

Summary

Long-term success in business requires companies to prevent problems from reaching the customer. This is especially important in the areas of performance, reliability, durability, and serviceability. Three formal tools for problem prevention are *specification development and review, statistical process control,* and *reliability emphasis.*

The team approach to specification development and review raises awareness of customer needs, increases accuracy of specs, and minimizes changes during production. Involving suppliers,

> *Block diagrams are a dynamite tool in improving the reliability of our products. We're able to isolate purchased parts needing improvement and take action. After you identify the subsystems and their associated parts, the math is easy (.99 x .914 x .869 x .951 = .748). In our example, there is a 74.8% chance that this product will perform for one year without a failure."*
> — Don

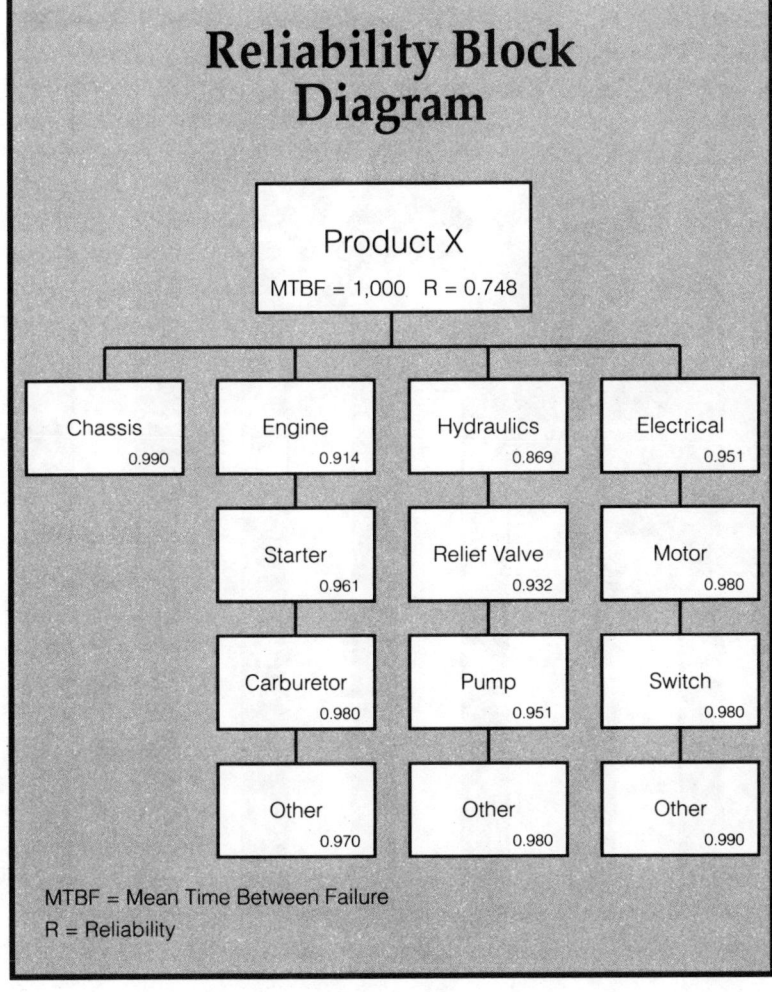

** *Our focused efforts are achieving substantial product reliability improvements . . . allowing us to earn customer loyalty."*
— Roger

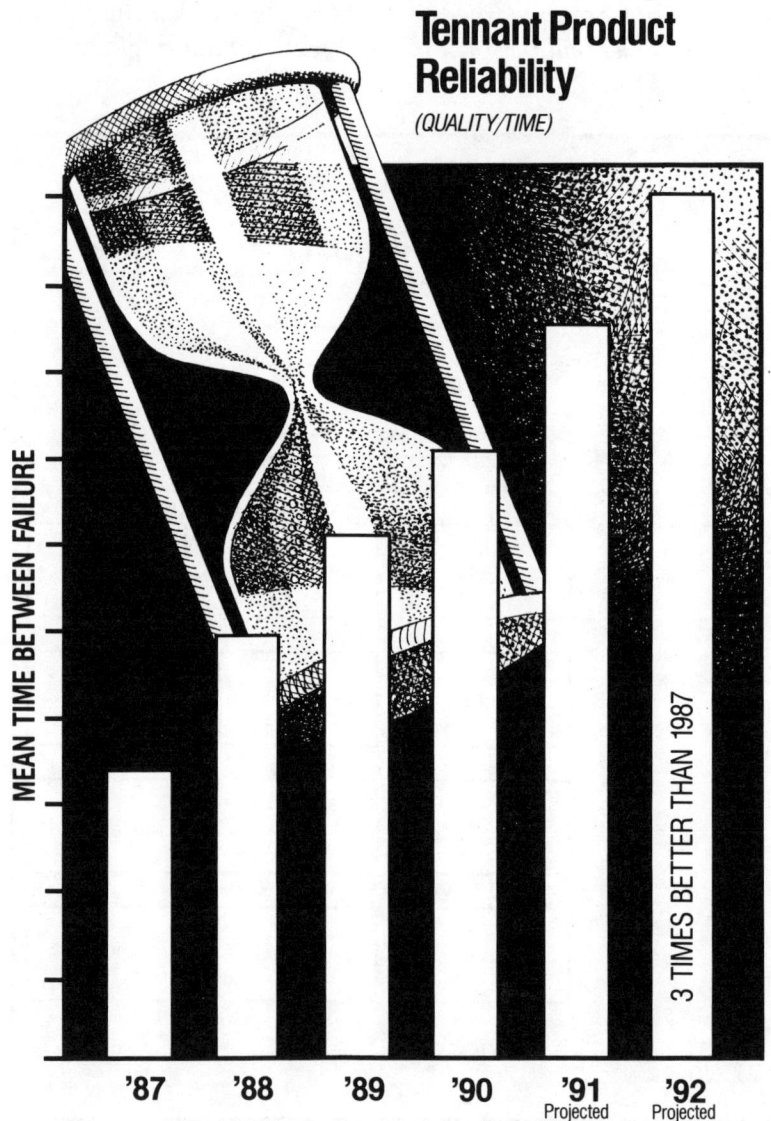

Tennant Product Reliability
(QUALITY/TIME)

MEAN TIME BETWEEN FAILURE

'87 '88 '89 '90 '91 Projected '92 Projected

3 TIMES BETTER THAN 1987

purchasing, quality control, and other team members helps us "Do it right the first time." We identify preferred sources, unclear information, and arbitrary tolerances to improve the specs.

We also use a team approach to SPC and provide statistical training to a large spectrum of employees. We all learn that *variation is a given*. Process capability studies and capability reports are important tools.

Our reliability (quality over time) emphasis is another team-wielded statistical tool. Block diagrams, for example, have helped us plot the reliability of each part for every machine. Calculating the mean time between failure (MTBF) has shown us that our reliability has been improving steadily over the years, enabling us to extend our product warranties.

Reliability data is widely used in the real world by many customers, suppliers, and manufacturers. If suppliers are unaware of statistical measures of reliability, educate them. Help them see how 98 percent reliability is not good enough, that you need 99.999 percent.

Chapter 7
Measuring and Reporting Quality

Some companies accept cost overruns, blown schedules, or mountains of rework as facts of life. "You have to react to crises that come up," they say. "You can't plan for everything."

At Tennant, we're now better prepared than we once were. We can't plan for every unknown, but it helps to collect data. Cost overruns, for example, occur gradually — there's a cost buildup. If you're tracking the growth of actual costs against projections, the overrun won't come as a surprise. You can take early action to contain costs.

Nor should blown schedules come as a surprise. If you're tracking the project's progress, you know whether or not you're on schedule. In the same way, "mountains" of rework accumulate one piece at a time. Inspectors can trace the piece to its source and identify the problem, if you have the data.

In all three cases, there's a big "IF." A surprising amount of data is lost because it is never collected. Such data can be very helpful if only someone recognizes the need and takes the opportunity to collect it.

On the other hand, sometimes companies collect and store data, but never use it fully. For example, back in the early eighties we couldn't name our ten best suppliers, even though we had the answers in raw data in various forms and places throughout the company. We simply weren't *data conscious.* We weren't making use of what was available because we didn't consistently record it. Sometimes we didn't even know we had it.

Since that trying time, we've increased our awareness; we're wiser about collecting and using our data. We know how many suppliers we have, and we have information on all of them. We collect, input, and check data, and have it available for analysis. We know acceptance rates, defect rates, and delivery performance. Of our 500 suppliers, 120 are in a formal evaluation program. They represent a large chunk of Tennant's yearly purchases, and twice a year we give them performance feedback, based on our data analysis.

We're more knowledgeable about what is going on in our plants, from assembly to inspection to management. We're more aware of how to measure quality. Most importantly, we've learned that improving a supplier's data consciousness is essential to improving supplier quality.

Thus, the fifth critical success factor is to *measure and report quality*. As a customer, we give suppliers frequent, precise, and detailed feedback on their performance. We insist that suppliers measure quality, reliability, and delivery by continually collecting data. We want our suppliers to share our data consciousness. They must know what our feedback means, know their biggest problems, and be able to act on them as needed.

Our suppliers like getting performance reports from us; sometimes we're the only customer they hear from in such detail. As Chuck Carlson of Solar Plastics says, "It's helped us be more professional. It's all there in black and white. We know what we have to do."

Becoming Data Conscious

As we've found, it's vital that suppliers understand the importance of data analysis and reporting, as well as the process we use to evaluate their performance. Our process is:

▶ Recognizing opportunities to measure
▶ Measuring
▶ Formatting and analyzing
▶ Sharing data

Recognizing Opportunities to Measure

Once we began looking for opportunities to measure, we found them everywhere and we encouraged others to look for opportunities also. Now our people's data consciousness is evident throughout.

For example, in the past few years our material controllers have used measures of inventory levels to reduce costs. They report that purchased production inventory is down 52 percent in eight years without sacrificing quantity discounts. Another measure is freight costs: down more than 50 percent, because the traffic department negotiates rates with selected carriers and

> *All functional areas at Tennant are responsible for measuring and reporting their cost of quality. Translating the dollars to percent of sales allows purchasing to see a truer picture of the results of the supplier quality emphasis. Of course, we use a Pareto analysis to identify improvement areas."*
> — Ron

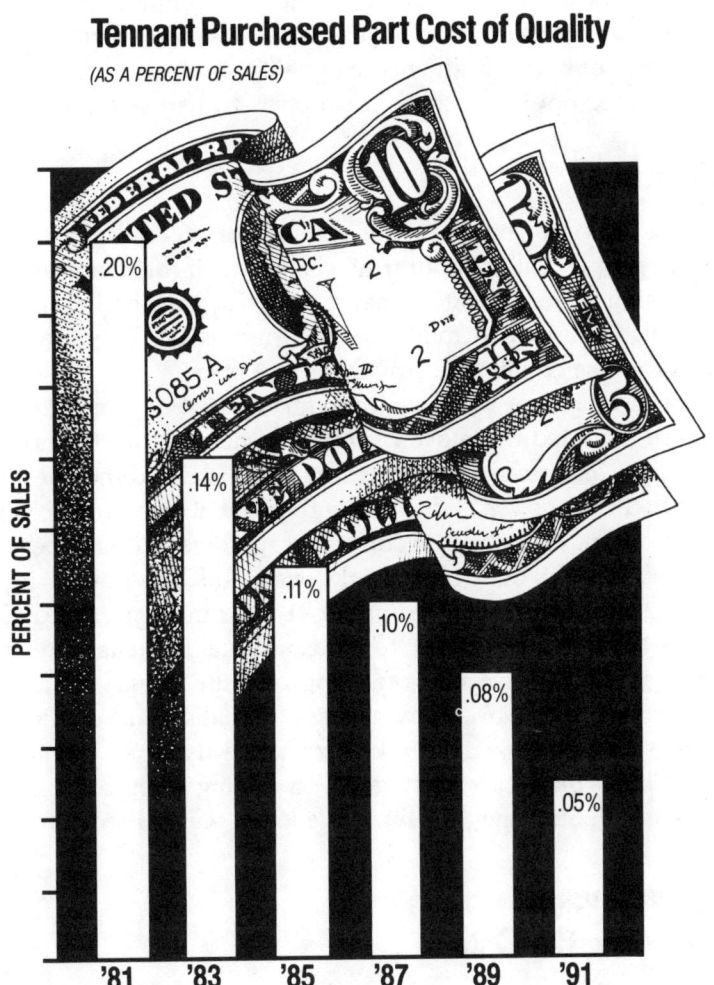

Tennant Purchased Part Cost of Quality
(AS A PERCENT OF SALES)

- '81: .20%
- '83: .14%
- '85: .11%
- '87: .10%
- '89: .08%
- '91: .05% (Projected)

materials control enforces supplier compliance. They also have a measure of customer service: our goal is to ship all service parts within 24 hours.

Tennant's assembly teams are also data conscious. For example, the Model 235 Small Rider Sweeper team used several measures to bring production closer to zero defects. The measures included: reduce hours per machine in assembly; reduce defects per machine; reduce loose hardware per machine; and achieve zero hydraulic leaks.

Suppliers are impressed to see how committed our people are to measuring and analyzing data. It's one more way we reinforce our commitment to quality and we set a good example for how we want our suppliers to handle data.

Measuring

Measuring may require a fair amount of creativity. In many cases, people will temporarily change their behavior if they know you're measuring — they try harder, or spend more time working — and you might get incorrect data. Thus, the best measures use counts that are already in place.

For example, a famous museum wanted to know which picture attracted the most visitors. Neither the curator nor the art expert had a clue. But when the janitors heard the question, they had the answer and the data to prove it: they replaced the tile in front of certain pictures every three months because patrons wore it out. They could even rank the popularity of the pictures, based on the amount of wear in the replaced tiles.

We think it's important to measure quality, reliability, and delivery. At first we had only approximate quality measures: on the line, our workers would say, "That's good quality" or "That's bad quality." We asked for more detail — quantification. "How many problems are you having with that pump?" we'd ask. "Lots!" they'd tell us. We knew we had work to do.

Formatting and Analyzing the Data

Once you have your measurements, the next task is to analyze

> *Our procurement specialists can measure the quality level of the suppliers they are responsible for on a monthly basis. By sharing this information with them, corrective action can be immediately taken. And the year-to-date report helps keep us on top of our biggest problems."*
> — Don

Purchased Material Nonconformance Report

Procurement Specialist: John French
Month: November

SUPPLIER NAME	NCR DATE	NCR QTY	PART NO.	PART DESCRIPTION	DEFECT DESCRIPTION	DISPO	SCRAP COST	CURRENT L&O COST
Cut Rate, Inc.	11–14	22	64211	Electric accessory	Missing threads	Scrap	44.09	11.49
	11–18	13	64211	Electric accessory	Will not operate	Rework	—	106.51
Subtotal							44.09	118.00
Hometown Mfg.	11–02	2	36409	Valve	Leaks externally	Rework	—	46.76
	11–24	6	36510	Support bracket	Cracked	Scrap	67.14	—
Subtotal							67.14	46.76
TOTAL							111.23	164.76

Supplier Cost of Quality Report

Year to Date: November

SUPPLIER NAME	YTD LABOR	YTD SCRAP	YTD TOTAL NCR COST	COSTS RECOVERED	YTD NET COST
Precision Ax Company	2,050.10	376.18	2,426.28	1,747.13	679.15
Hometown Mfg.	1,682.09	233.12	1,915.21	930.11	985.10
Circuit Master	824.48	460.83	1,285.31	750.67	534.64
Cut Rate, Inc.	523.49	0	523.49	376.59	146.90
Lazer Razer	117.72	0	117.72	46.00	71.72

the data. Reporting is nothing more than formatting output in such a way that you can present information effectively. Our reports have several purposes. They tell us our biggest problems with purchased components and suppliers. We use them as a problem-resolution tool and as feedback for our suppliers. We also answer internal questions regarding hard costs, soft costs, rework, and scrap reimbursement. And we produce our reliability performance reports, discussed earlier.

Sharing Data With Suppliers

Based on each supplier's information, we do six-month quality update reports, listing the goals we've set with the supplier, as well as their performance. We specifically note whether or not they met the goals.

The quality update report summarizes the supplier's performance in the areas of quality, delivery, and reliability. The measurements support every conclusion and recommendation made in the quality update. By reporting and analyzing the data, we directly contribute to our product quality and to enhancing the quality of our suppliers.

It is important to be cordial and complimentary, but we also want to let the suppliers know exactly what we need. Most important, the data we collect and share enables the supplier to put improvement action plans in place. The letters and quality updates we send are often very high-visibility items and we have discovered that supplier top management takes them very seriously.

Summary

Measuring and reporting quality is a vital part of establishing quality suppliers. Companies may be collecting a great deal of data, but much of it is escaping unnoticed and unanalyzed. By establishing data consciousness in your own operation, and in your suppliers, you can improve their quality. The four processes involved are: recognizing opportunities to measure, measuring, formatting and analyzing data, and sharing data.

> *The letters to our suppliers are short and to the point. We like to see responses that show both improvement goals and action plans."*
> — Tim

Dear Supplier:

Enclosed are your performance level status reports in the areas of product quality and delivery covering the period from July through December. In reviewing your recent results, please note how you are doing compared to previous reporting periods and to Tennant Company's required goals for "Qualified" supplier status:

	Our Goals	Your Performance
Zero defects on piece parts	99.9%	98.0%
Incoming lots accepted	100%	93.9%
On-time delivery	100%	100%

Please provide me with your 1991 performance goals for all three categories. At this time, you are still considered "Conditionally Qualified." I would like to add your company to our elite group of "Qualified Suppliers" in 1992. With a little extra effort, I believe you can do it.

Very truly yours,

Dear Tennant:

We have reviewed the quality data that you enclosed in your recent letter, outlining our performance levels. We did not meet all your goals, but we're confident we'll do better over the next reporting period.

A statistical process control program is being implemented in our plant next month. Our management and supervisory personnel have already been trained and our plant employees are being trained now. Plus, our suppliers are being brought into our quality emphasis.

These combined efforts will provide us with substantial results. So, we're pleased to submit our lot acceptance goal and piece part goal at 100% and 99.9% respectively.

Sincerely,

With practice and effort, everyone in a company can be data conscious. The end goal, as with everything we do, is to satisfy our customers by making a better product. Good data is a trouble-shooting tool for us and for our suppliers. As one supplier says, "If *you're* having problems with our parts, chances are *our other customers* are, too. The sooner we know the problem, the sooner we can get to a solution."

Chapter 8
Qualifying Suppliers

Communication is vital when establishing an understanding about quality with suppliers. In fact, if you don't communicate effectively, a lot of hard work will be for naught. We talk with our suppliers at every opportunity. We suggest you do the same.

Make visits, call on the telephone, send letters. Make extraordinary efforts. Share information: educate your suppliers in what you want, and train them to produce it. Provide feedback on their performance — certificates, reports, and commendations. Recognize them. Invite them to meetings. Show them you think they're important.

Remember: suppliers may initially question, even test, your commitment to quality. That was the case when we began our quality emphasis. Don recalls that "At first a lot of people thought quality was just another buzzword. Then they saw that we did much more than simply talk about it. We lived it, breathed it, performed it — to a point where Tennant became synonymous with quality."

Let suppliers know what you want, ask them to help you get it, and tell them you will reward them when they do. Talk to as many of their employees as you can, from top management to quality control to assemblers. Most of what we've been saying in this book focuses on communicating with suppliers.

And the message to give them? At Tennant we share our supplier qualification requirements and the need to meet them. In fact, the sixth critical success factor is *qualifying suppliers*. We want suppliers who exhibit a strong desire to be qualified. We require them to meet qualification criteria within a specified time and maintain it throughout the relationship. As we've discussed before, we expect them to deliver on their commitments to us, their customer, according to our expectations.

Supplier Qualification Criteria

At Tennant, we've developed eight specific criteria by which we identify and qualify our suppliers:

▶ On-site supplier assessment

- Management involvement
- Mutual understanding of requirements
- Supplier corrective action request system
- Reliability performance
- Incoming lot performance
- Piece part performance
- Delivery performance

The first four criteria are interactive items: we visit, we talk, we establish mutual understanding, we see how they will work with us to prevent and correct problems. The second four criteria are the measurement items discussed in previous chapters: suppliers commit to quality performance as measured by these yardsticks.

We will describe each of these criteria below, after discussing the supplier qualification categories.

Supplier Qualification Categories

Our purchasing department explains the criteria to the potential supplier and then evaluates them. We classify suppliers into one of three categories:

- Qualified
- Conditionally qualified
- Unqualified

In working with suppliers, we expect to improve our communications, not only in quality management, but throughout all aspects of our relationship. We look for improvement every year. Our long-range goal: to do business only with qualified suppliers.

Qualified suppliers are the best: they meet all eight criteria. New business is assigned to qualified suppliers before seeking other sources. We reassign existing business to them as practical. We agree with Tom Runyon, a senior procurement specialist at Tennant, who calls our qualified suppliers "silent

" The Carrier Qualification process was developed by Teresa Frazee, Tennant traffic manager, to find and use carriers who meet our quality and compatibility requirements. According to Teresa, our incoming and outgoing freight carriers should be selected, measured, and held accountable for their performance like our production parts suppliers. And I happen to agree with her."

— Don

TENNANT CARRIER QUALIFICATION AND EVALUATION

The Carrier Qualification criteria includes:
- Financial stability as judged by balance sheets and statements of income
- Compatibility of equipment to TENNANT products
- Conformance to TENNANT tariff and class exception guidelines
- Distribution system compatible with TENNANT standards
- Ability to handle freezable materials
- Electronic data interchange
- Claims history

		Maximum Points			Maximum Points
I.	CLAIMS	20	VI.	FREEZABLES	0
II.	BILLING ACCURACY	10	VII.	PICKUPS	0
III.	SERVICE	20	VIII.	CUSTOMER SERVICE	10
IV.	PRICING	20	IX.	FINANCIAL STABILITY	5
V.	SERVICE REPORT	5		Total points possible each month	90

Carriers will be classified into one of the following categories using the evaluation criteria established for the type of carrier:

1. *Select carrier* is the highest rating that a carrier can obtain. To achieve this status, a carrier must consistently attain 900+ points annually. Select carriers will be given an option to bid on any new lanes of traffic before preferred or qualified carriers.
2. A *Preferred carrier* consistently meets most criteria and has demonstrated a desire to improve performance in areas of weakness. To achieve preferred carrier status, a carrier must attain 800–900 points annually in the evaluation process.
3. A *Qualified carrier* has met with initial qualification criteria but has not demonstrated preferred or select carrier standards.
4. A *Non–Qualified carrier* has not met the initial qualification criteria.

heroes." As Tom says, "They come through for us over and over, job after job, with no problems."

Conditionally qualified suppliers meet most, but not all of the criteria. We tell these suppliers exactly what conditions they must satisfy before becoming qualified and how much time they have to do it. If they don't meet our criteria, they risk becoming unqualified. We do not assign new business to these suppliers if we have qualified suppliers who can provide the parts.

Unqualified suppliers are neither performing at acceptable levels nor are they improving. They get no new business from Tennant, and we dissolve the relationship if they don't improve after a reasonable period. Frankly, some suppliers just don't think it's worth the trouble to improve. You're better off without them.

Our approach to qualifying suppliers has worked so well, we're now applying similar criteria to other areas. For example, Tennant has a carrier qualification process to assure that carriers meet our standards for quality and compatibility. Carriers are rated from "select" to "nonqualified" and get Tennant business accordingly. It's our long-term goal to work only with select carriers.

On-Site Supplier Assessment

Our first step in the supplier qualification process involves an on-site assessment jointly conducted by purchasing and quality assurance. We usually spend one full day at the supplier's site, examining the following areas:

- ▶ Quality Systems
  - Are quality measurements and goals displayed?
  - Does the supplier track reliability performance?
  - Are production operations promptly shut down when problems are discovered?
- ▶ Organization
  - Who does the quality staff report to?

- Who is the contact person in each key functional area?
▶ Market Analysis
- Describe the market scope of business, key markets served, and market position.

▶ Financial Analysis
- Review annual report, 10-K report, D&B, etc.
- Long-term debt as a percent of total assets?
- R & D spending as a percent of sales?

▶ Operating Systems
- Walk through and describe in detail the steps taken, paper and material flow, when a request for quote, purchase order, and product change order are received.
- Are drawings and specifications on a CAD data base? Can they be electronically transferred to us?

▶ Support Capabilities
- Do field engineers conduct training seminars?
- Can our product be tested at the supplier's facility?

▶ Policies
- What is the Warranty/Returned Goods policy?
- What is the Rework Labor Reimbursement policy?
- What are typical lead times and firm periods?

▶ Manufacturing Assessment
- Is a Productivity Improvement Plan in place?
- Is there a logical start and finish to work flow with no apparent backtracking?
- Are setup methods efficient (quick clamping, minimum tools, etc.)?
- Is there a place for everything and everything in its place?

Lance Larson, Tennant's director of product development and research, believes these on-site visits are one of the best ways we have to help suppliers feel like an extension of Tennant. "When you're in the supplier's plant, you suddenly matter more," Lance says, echoing a thought we've all had when visiting a supplier. "You're not a voice over the phone. You see their operation, see what they have to deal with."

Supplier Management Involvement

The second step in Tennant's supplier qualification process requires the involvement of supplier top management. We accomplish this in a number of ways. In the early years, we brought supplier executives in for formal meetings; quality was the only item on the agenda. Today, those meetings have evolved to where we discuss all aspects of our business relationship. We establish a relationship during the initial meeting that will continue and grow, and involve our own top management with theirs from the start. We discuss our zero defects process and the important role that our suppliers play in our business — well over half of every machine we produce is made up of supplier parts.

One of our suppliers' executives admits he didn't take the quality emphasis seriously until Tennant visited his headquarters. "Sitting across the table from the Tennant people, it was obvious they were committed to quality and we were a bit shaky," he recalls. "It was embarrassing. You can't argue with the goal of producing a quality product."

Having top management commitment works every time. Ed Sabraski, one of Tennant's senior quality engineers, remembers when every valve we bought from a certain supplier needed rework. We were about to drop the supplier when their top management saw the light on quality. They made a commitment to improve and said, "please work with us." Six months later they were up to 95 percent zero defects; a year later, they'd made 99 percent. As Ed says, "If you have that management commitment, you can do just about anything — if you don't have it, you can't do a thing."

Mutual Understanding of Requirements

Tennant's supplier qualification process also emphasizes a mutual understanding of requirements. We want our requirements to be clear and understandable to suppliers, and we

" We think it's important to go over as much detail as possible with our suppliers so they will clearly understand how we conduct the purchasing part of our business. Copies of the manual are always left with them. Overall, this process helps get new relationships off to a good start and solidifies others."
— Ron

SUPPLIER REQUIREMENTS AND INFORMATION MANUAL

PURPOSE

At TENNANT, we consider suppliers to be an integral part of a companywide effort to attain product excellence and reliability within our competitive markets. The importance of a supplier's role in providing quality materials and processing cannot be overstated. We welcome new ideas and expect supplier suggestions to achieve lower costs and better values.

This booklet defines performance levels TENNANT expects from its suppliers and describes company policies and practices affecting our relationship with them. Communication devices for monitoring performance, for implementing these policies, and for defining responsibilities involved are explained and described.

CONTENTS

1. **INTRODUCTION**
   - Purpose 1
   - TENNANT Background 1
   - TENNANT Quality 2
   - Supplier Quality Goals 3
2. **TENNANT PURCHASED MATERIAL MANAGEMENT**
   - Purchasing Organization and Responsibility................. 3
   - Materials Organization and Responsibility................. 3
   - Request for Quotation Process 4
   - Purchase Orders 4
   - Delivery Requirements 5
   - Transportation 5
   - Packaging of Materials........... 5
   - Aftermarket/Service Parts Requirements................. 6
   - Invoicing 6
   - Minority and Disadvantaged Businesses................... 7
   - Ethics............................ 7
   - Confidentiality 7
3. **SUPPLIER QUALITY ASSURANCE REQUIREMENTS**
   - Quality Control System........... 7
   - Organization 7
   - Design and Process Change Control 7
   - Procedures 8
   - Inspection and Testing 8
   - Measurement and Test Equipment .. 8
   - Control of Subcontracted Supplies .. 8
   - Quality Documentation........... 9
   - Quality Status Identification 9
   - Special Requirements for Distributors.................... 9
4. **TENNANT QUALITY ASSURANCE PROCESS**
   - Supplier Qualification 10
   - Materials Qualification 10
   - Receiving Inspection 11
   - Non-Standard Reporting System 11
   - Supplier Corrective Action Team 11
   - Disposition of Defective Material ...11
   - Returning Defective Material 11
   - Supplier Corrective Action Request .12
5. **APPENDICES**
   - A. Purchase Order................13
   - B. Supplier Corrective Action Request 15
   - C. Return for Replacement or Credit 17
   - D. TENNANT Drawing 19

115

want their requirements to be clear and understandable to us. Conformance to requirements is a key to quality.

We also go over our "Supplier Requirements and Information Manual" with suppliers, as a basis to talk about our requirements. It's a communication tool rather than a definitive guide, but it gets us talking.

Supplier Corrective Action Request System

Corrective action requests are also a vital factor in qualifying Tennant suppliers. We want the supplier to understand the process. We also want to know: to whom to send the form, that someone will feel a sense of urgency when they receive it, and that all requests will be answered within the specified time.

Reliability Performance

We recognize the importance of reliability in the quest for quality. Basically, reliability means the product will perform according to specifications throughout its expected life. Reliability is measurable and we expect that our qualified suppliers will commit to work with us in this area. By helping each other we both improve our product reliability.

Incoming Lot Acceptance

Yet another consideration in qualifying suppliers is incoming lot acceptance. We expect 12 months or 100 consecutive lots of 100 percent acceptance. This was a much more necessary measurement in our early stages than it is today. Supplier performance has improved, and we no longer do incoming inspections on most parts.

Piece Part Performance

Qualified suppliers must also set goals toward achieving zero defects on parts used in our manufacturing process. Suppliers must meet our goal for number of defect-free parts used in production during a reporting period. Each commodity has a set goal, and the goal gradually increases toward zero defects as the commodity improves. We also expect suppliers to set individual company goals as evidence they are continually improving.

Recognizing the various complexity levels of purchased components, we have different performance goals for different commodities. For example:

Group	Defect Goal	Examples of Commodities
I	1 per 1000	Hydraulic hoses and fittings, bearings, rubber, decals
II	4 per 1000	Electrical devices, wheels and tires, formed parts, plastics
III	10 per 1000	Engines, electric motors, hydraulics

Delivery Performance

On-time delivery is also a criteria for qualifying suppliers. Early shipments cost extra because of warehousing and inventory buildup. Late shipments can shut production down. We expect the supplier to meet our goal of 100 percent on-time delivery — not early, not late.

Materials Controller Curt Lange notes that our delivery performance reports have improved communications in an unexpected way. "Now suppliers let us know ahead of time if they'll be late with a delivery," he notes. "Before we did the reports, no one told us anything! Now we have time to adjust."

Recognition

We've never met anyone who doesn't appreciate recognition for a job well done. That's why we're very careful to acknowledge suppliers who are consistently outstanding. We want all members of the supplier's team to know we appreciate their efforts. We go for maximum impact. It's fun to arrange a celebration to recognize an outstanding supplier.

At Tennant our awards are meaningful partly because we don't give out many. We're very selective — recognizing only those suppliers with whom all aspects of our relationship are outstanding. Award recipients must meet the qualification criteria over a specified period of time. Then they must be nominated by a member of our procurement team who has dealt with them and appreciates their efforts in all aspects of the business relationship. Finally, purchasing management must approve the choice.

Once the supplier is selected to receive an award, we prepare a special recognition plaque. We never present a plaque that says "Qualified Supplier" since we are always reevaluating the status of our suppliers. We don't want someone with a "Qualified Supplier" plaque in the lobby and a lot of failure reports on their desks.

Not all recognition has to be formal. John Schlegel from Ford still chuckles when he tells about the cartoon we had made up for one of his visits to Tennant. "I was fully expecting to get beat up real bad," he recalls. "I expected a negative — we'd been having some delivery problems — but instead I get this wonderful drawing with Ford motors coming out of the gates of heaven. I came home motivated to do a better job."

Summary

In this chapter we have discussed criteria for qualifying suppliers and the importance of frequent communication with them, from top management to quality control to assemblers, especially about quality and qualification criteria.

We reviewed the eight criteria we use to qualify suppliers:

On-Site Supplier Assessment. We visit the supplier site and look at a list of specific items, such as quality systems, organization, market analysis, financial analysis, operating systems, support capabilities, policies, and manufacturing.

Supplier Management Involvement. We bring top management in for a meeting and involve our top management with theirs from the start to establish our business relationship. We let them know they play an important role in our business and secure their commitment to quality.

Mutual Understanding of Requirements. We review our "Supplier Requirements and Information Manual" and make sure they understand our requirements, and we understand theirs.

Supplier Corrective Action Requests. We introduce our supplier corrective action request system, so they understand the process and so they will place a sense of urgency on responding.

Reliability. We explain the importance of reliability, establish our measures of it, and ask for the supplier's commitment.

Incoming Lot Acceptance. We explain our requirement that they provide 12 months or 100 consecutive lots that are acceptable.

Piece Part Performance. We explain our performance goals for different commodities and ask them to set goals toward achieving zero defects.

Delivery Performance. We explain the importance of on-time delivery and how we expect the supplier to meet our goal of 100 percent on-time delivery.

Finally, we discussed the importance of recognition — we feel it is important to recognize outstanding suppliers. We provide formal and informal recognition, but never a plaque that says "Qualified Supplier" because we are always reevaluating their status.

Chapter 9

Annual Business Management Sessions

Now, for the most important part of the book — taking all the components we've discussed and putting them into a structure that assures supplier quality. At Tennant we've learned that formalizing our approach to supplier quality is essential. We've developed a format we call *Annual Business Management Sessions*, our seventh critical success factor in the development of suppliers. We have carefully developed our objectives, strategy, and the overall process.

Corporate Objective. We have a precise objective for our supplier sessions: to work toward continuous quality improvement and aggressive cost containment.

The Strategy. We have worked out a strategy to achieve that objective. First, we establish that engineering, manufacturing, and purchasing have a common goal. We want to work together to improve quality and contain costs. Second, we concentrate on purchased components. We strive to design with fewer parts, use common parts across our product line, and use suppliers' standard parts whenever we can. We also design with different materials — plastic instead of steel.

With our top 50 suppliers (who represent 70 percent of our purchases), we hold major meetings involving many people from both our organization and theirs — top management, engineering, purchasing, and others who may have helpful information. It's an in-depth meeting that involves a great deal of advance planning on both sides.

With the next 50 suppliers, we work in mini-management sessions, usually including Tennant purchasing people and sales management from suppliers as the highest level of participation. Finally, we work in one-on-one sessions with our remaining suppliers; these are simpler sessions, often between the supplier's rep and the Tennant procurement specialist on that account.

These business management sessions are a crucial part of Tennant's supplier quality emphasis: we develop a formal schedule of meetings each year and individual procurement specialists have, as part of their job goals, the responsibility to make them happen.

The Process. We take our meetings with suppliers very seriously. These meetings are one of our main communication devices with their top management. If we are addressing problems in meeting goals, we want top management to be aware of the situation.

The procurement specialist coordinates and conducts the in-house rehearsal meeting, pulls all information together for all participants, and works out a detailed plan. When we make the supplier visit, the procurement specialist is in charge of coordinating the actual business management session. He or she is completely familiar with all facets of the account as well as with our strategy for the meeting.

Our annual business management sessions progress through five stages:

- ▶ Preparation
- ▶ Rehearsal
- ▶ Agenda
- ▶ Meeting
- ▶ Summary Letter

Notice that the actual meeting is the fourth stage in the process. A great deal of effort goes into making sure the meeting has a win/win outcome for both Tennant and our supplier.

Preparation

In preparing for these sessions, our procurement specialist puts together a "situation analysis." This involves researching and summarizing the history of our dealings with the supplier. It also involves describing the current "state of affairs" concerning us and the supplier.

After looking carefully at all aspects of our history with a supplier, we analyze the situation. We ask the following questions of ourselves: What is going on with this supplier? Are we happy with their progress? Are there problems? Are we causing them problems? How can we improve the relationship and help each other achieve our objectives?

Casting Stones

Cessna Fluid Power Company was one of the first 15 suppliers invited in to talk to us about quality (1981). The agenda for the meeting included a presentation of our quality history and our future improvement goals.

I listed all the defects we had experienced with their parts in 1979 and 1980. I specifically pointed out "binding" valve spools as the major problem with their parts. I asked what they were going to do to correct the problem and get us good parts.

Later, during a plant tour, I showed the group where we sub-assembled the valves prior to final machine assembly. It was at that time Cessna pointed out how Tennant was incorrectly using a vice to hold the valves in place for the sub-assembly operation. Our mistake caused the castings to be distorted which made the spools bind.

It was a very embarrassing moment for me, but it clearly pointed out that we caused many of the so-called "supplier" problems ourselves. This experience continues to reinforce the importance of ongoing business meetings with our suppliers.

— Tim

> *The Supplier Satisfaction Rating Form is jointly completed during our rehearsal meetings with everyone in attendance providing input. It's important to share this information with suppliers as part of their performance review. We are totally committed to working with suppliers in any way we can to help them achieve excellent ratings in all categories."*
> — Ron

(TENNANT) SUPPLIER SATISFACTION RATING

Supplier: _____ Qualified: ☐ Yes ☐ No

Commodity _____ Product _____

I. General Impression

	Excellent	Good	Average	Poor
A. How well does this supplier meet TENNANT's quality expectations?	___	___	___	___

B. How well do they meet our expectations in the following areas?

	Excellent	Good	Average	Poor
1. Product reliability	___	___	___	___
2. Sales support	___	___	___	___
3. Technical service	___	___	___	___
4. Customer service support	___	___	___	___
5. On-time delivery	___	___	___	___
6. Cost containment	___	___	___	___
7. Terms of payment	___	___	___	___
8. Warranty policy	___	___	___	___
9. Return goods policy	___	___	___	___
10. SCAR response	___	___	___	___
11. Top management involvement	___	___	___	___

II. Customer Satisfaction

A. Sales Representation

	Excellent	Good	Average	Poor

How well does sales representation meet our expectations?

	Excellent	Good	Average	Poor
1. Frequency of contact	___	___	___	___
2. Provide information on new products and services	___	___	___	___
3. Product knowledge	___	___	___	___
4. Problem solving	___	___	___	___
5. Professionalism	___	___	___	___
6. Prompt call backs	___	___	___	___
7. Accessibility	___	___	___	___

		Excellent	Good	Average	Poor

B. Delivery Administration

How well do they meet our expectations on purchase orders and delivery?

1. Meet promise dates
2. Expediting follow-up
3. Schedule change flexibility
4. Shipment accuracy
5. Invoice accuracy
6. Packaging

C. Engineering Support

How well do they meet our Engineering Support expectations?

1. Knowledge of our applications
2. Share R & D plans
3. Technical expertise
4. Technical support
5. Detail exactness
6. Promptness
7. Overall responsiveness

D. Cost Containment

How well does this supplier work with us in containing costs?

1. Controls price increases
2. Innovative in cost reductions
3. Advance notice of price increases
4. Pricing activity justification
5. Long-term pricing commitments
6. Repair parts
7. Provides cost breakdown
8. Performance vs. inflation

III. Comments

Other areas to address to mutually improve our customer/supplier relationship?

We also consider whether our volume of business with the supplier is increasing or decreasing. We review the highlights of previous meetings: did we accomplish previous goals? We review the supplier's performance on quality, delivery, reliability and cost containment. We compare the supplier's price performance with economic indicators and with other suppliers' performance on similar commodities.

Rehearsal

We conduct a dry run of the business management session at our home office, with everyone attending who might have information about the supplier. These people may include:

- Tennant executive
- Design engineer
- Corporate procurement manager
- Procurement engineering manager
- Procurement specialist
- Material controller
- Quality engineer

At the rehearsal meeting, we work as a group, reviewing the situation regarding the supplier, including recent performance compared to goals. All variables relating to customer/supplier relationship are explored, looking for mutually beneficial improvement opportunities.

We then determine which employees will attend the meeting, and what their roles will be. We decide what will be presented and we prioritize agenda items. Finally we discuss what each person will present and what we want to accomplish in the meeting.

For example, we need a meeting facilitator, a note taker, and specific individuals with working knowledge of the issues. It is imperative that this group has authority to make decisions on the spot. We don't want to meet just to schedule a second meeting.

Agenda

We structure the meeting to be sure we cover all necessary

issues. Therefore, we develop a formal agenda, with supplier input, listing the assigned roles. We publish this agenda ahead of time, so that the supplier knows what we expect. Our communication lines are always open so that nothing we say in these annual meetings comes as a surprise. We never want to blindside our suppliers.

"Prepare" is the key word. We do our homework ahead of time, and we expect our suppliers to do the same. We don't hold these meetings simply to raise issues; we want to resolve issues, develop an action plan. A typical agenda might be:

- ▶ Tennant and Supplier Business Overview: Past, Current, and Future
- ▶ Supplier Quality Performance
  - Delivery
  - Quality
  - Reliability
  - Supplier Qualification Status
- ▶ Technical Product Issues Discussion
- ▶ Tennant Cost Containment Objectives, Strategies, and Supplier's Responsibility
- ▶ Future Action Plan and Mutual Business Commitment Discussion

Of course, other topics will also be discussed, including: opportunities to consolidate business; Tennant provided training assistance; just-in-time; information technology applications; improvement goals, and more.

The Meeting

In most cases, we have found it helpful to rotate locations. We might meet at the supplier's site one year, at Tennant the next.

We try to stick to the agenda as much as possible — it was carefully planned for maximum impact, and we want to cover everything. However, it's also important to be flexible. If the supplier has special concerns, deal with them.

Be prepared to miss your flight. Maximize your impact while you have the opportunity. Don't be handcuffed to a flight schedule. If problems arise and you have to work out con-

> *It's crucial to document the meeting highlights of the business management session. Be sure that commitments are followed up. Remember, this year's highlight letter will be on next year's agenda and no one wants to be embarrassed by lack of action."*
> — Don

Dear Supplier:

I'd like to take this opportunity to thank you and your staff for the hospitality provided us during our annual business management session. I feel these meetings are extremely productive and very worthwhile. The following are the commitments and responsibilities we agreed to:

- We will work jointly on a value analysis package that will include material gauge reduction, returnable crates and electronic order processing.
- Tennant will provide your test lab with a walk-behind scrubber for reliability testing of your components in this machine.
- You will work directly with our Tennant operations in the Netherlands in an effort to provide parts directly or through your European affiliate.
- You agreed to reduce your lead time and firm periods from 16 to 12 weeks and nine weeks to four weeks, respectively.
- You accepted a yearly blanket order with releases spread over 12 months.
- Tennant agreed to a three-year business commitment with you. We will provide you some consolidation opportunities.
- You agreed to reduce your prices by 10 percent over the next three years and to extend your warranties to two years.

Again, thanks for the time you spent in accommodating us. If I left anything out, please let me know.

Best regards,

flicts — work them out. It's also important to let suppliers know exactly where they stand. We present the facts exactly as we know them, never glossed over or watered down.

Conflict is not necessarily a negative thing. It's bound to occur now and then: discussions can get tense as you make your quality expectations clear. At Tennant, we want to work through those issues so we can continue to develop a long-term relationship based on trust and mutual respect. We all remember times when we've called a time-out and asked to huddle or caucus with our team. If surprises come up, take time to discuss them with your colleagues, then go back to the meeting, prepared to be candid. There's no point in trying to bluff your way through. As we've said before, the purpose of this meeting is to solve problems, not to schedule another meeting.

Take good notes. As the agenda unfolds, note each point, reactions, agreements, questions, action items. This meeting is a key aspect of your relations with this supplier for at least the next year. Record the important details. When the meeting is over, be ready to summarize the key issues, outcomes, and action plans. This summary serves as a check on everyone's understanding and responsibilities. At the end, we want everyone involved to feel good about the outcome.

Don't expect everything to happen at once. As one of our major suppliers recalls, "Our relationship with Tennant improved gradually. Now, after several years, we share so much that we've had Tennant people sit in on business management sessions with *our* raw material suppliers. We've never done that with another customer."

Summary Letter

The summary letter concludes the annual business management session process. Use your notes and the recollections of others when writing the letter. Summarize the highlights. List what was discussed, as you understand it. Describe the commitments you've both made. Write out the agreed-upon action plan. Be specific on what date things should be done and who is specifically responsible. Communicate your expectations.

Finally, follow up on your commitments and follow up with

the supplier on theirs. Send out progress reports to let others know how everyone is doing on their action plans. Take the initiative to make things happen. Maintain the partnership.

Summary

The Annual Business Management Sessions are a key aspect of communicating with suppliers. At Tennant, we spend many hours planning for the sessions. Alerting the supplier to our expectations for the meeting is a professional courtesy; we never want to blindside them. During the meeting, we follow the planned agenda, take time-outs to discuss "surprise" situations with our team, and view conflict as an inevitable part of the relationship-building process. We always send a letter summarizing the meeting and, most importantly, we live up to our commitments, and we follow up with suppliers to be sure they do the same. There is no doubt that Tennant and our suppliers benefit greatly from these very candid sessions.

Section III

Go for It!

Throughout this book, we've shared with you some of the things that work exceptionally well for us in the area of supplier performance. The quality of the parts and services we buy today is at an all-time high. The relationships we enjoy with our suppliers are second to none.

Tennant continues to be recognized as a premier quality company worldwide, and the very important role our suppliers play in this recognition can't be overemphasized. We are confident we are on the right track. We've made a lot of progress and we're proud of that.

However, we are very quick to recognize, in the whole scheme of things, that our journey has just begun. Incremental improvements may have been acceptable in the eighties, but they will not be enough to survive in the nineties.

Significant improvements will be needed in product quality and reliability. Much more frequent deliveries will be demanded, and anything less than exactly on-time will be intolerable. Product development times must be slashed throughout the entire chain — from concept, design tooling, prototypes, and production. And, of course, thoroughly understanding the needs of customers and responding quickly and effectively to them, believe it or not, will have to become commonplace.

The progress we've made up to this point has not been easy. We have expended a tremendous amount of effort and we've been working at it for a long time. Meeting the challenges of the future will be even more difficult. But we intend to take them on.

At the same time, we don't expect overnight results. By being tenacious in our supplier quality emphasis, our purchased parts and services will continue to get better and better. And this will enable Tennant to provide our customers with superior products and services, year after year.

We hope you have learned and benefited from our story. And, as you consider how our strategies might apply to your unique business situation, we would like to suggest that you try something that has worked interestingly well for the hundreds of business people who have attended our supplier quality workshops: share this book with four or five of your colleagues, your staff, and others who are concerned about quality. Then set aside a few hours to complete the following case study.

You'll soon find yourselves emotionally and intellectually involved in the issues we've examined in this book. From there, you can continue your quality journey.

Chapter 10
A Case Study

For the next few hours, you will be employed by the E.Z. Skate Company, a manufacturer of ice resurfacing equipment used to maintain a smooth surface on ice skating rinks. The disposable "ice blade," which shaves the top layer off, is one of the most critical components of your equipment. It's expensive to replace and represents significant after-market business for you.

Customers demand that the blade be perfect; a nicked or crooked blade means an uneven shave — skaters fall and hockey pucks "weave" on the ice. Your design engineers have been redesigning the blade for some time. They want to make it faster and easier to replace and they want a cutting edge that provides a cleaner, smoother shave. They also want a sharper blade, one that will shave the ice fast. Rink operators are demanding a new blade: it will save them maintenance time and increase their income by giving them more ice time to sell.

You will purchase the new blade, as you do the current one. In fact, you've been working with two suppliers simultaneously throughout the design, development, and prototype stages. One is your current supplier, Precision Ax Company, from whom you've been buying blades for 11 years. The other is Lazer Razer, Inc., a company you haven't dealt with before.

You want a single source and it's now time to decide who gets the blade business. You and your colleagues have had many discussions with representatives of both suppliers during the design stage. The next step in the selection process is to have your representatives meet with the supplier representatives in a business management session.

Your purchasing manager has called a "rehearsal" meeting to prepare for one of these sessions. The following employees will be included:

► Purchasing manager
► Design engineer
► Quality/reliability technician
► Vice president, manufacturing, engineering and purchasing

Roles

You'll each play a specific role during the rehearsal. Choose your role from one of the following:

Purchasing Manager. You prefer to give the new blade business to your current supplier, Precision Ax Company. You've been working with them for a long time and you think the supplier/customer relationship is pretty good.

Whenever needed, Precision Ax has responded to your requests. That's been especially valuable since they've been a bit inconsistent on deliveries and somewhat unpredictable on quality. Even though they make some mistakes, you're impressed that they're quick to fix them and get you your product.

They've also been responsive throughout the design and development stages of the new blade — not particularly proactive in providing technical expertise to your design engineering group, but they've provided prototypes according to the prints you've given them. You think they would give you a satisfactory product.

You're equally confident that Lazer Razer could be a good supplier, but you don't want to add someone new. You also don't want to damage your relationship with Precision Ax because you buy other products from them in addition to blades.

You also have to admit that you're a bit offended that Lazer Razer's rep continually goes around you and deals directly with your design engineer. In fact, the design engineer brought Lazer Razer in; they worked together at another company years ago.

Percent On-time Delivery Performance for Precision Ax

1981	1982	1983	1984	1985	1986	1987	1988	1989	1990
84	92	90	93	91	89	93	93	94	92

Design Engineer. You would really like to give the business to Lazer Razer. They've been helpful in designing the new blade and you're impressed with the technological expertise they bring to the table. They routinely challenge your ideas by presenting their own. They've stimulated your creative juices and you have a better product because of it.

On the other hand, Precision Ax hasn't volunteered any ideas or challenged any of the prints you gave them. They're a bit too passive and reactive for your tastes. They can probably produce the new blade okay, but you'd like more out of the relationship. Besides, you don't think they should get the business just because they've been around for 11 years.

Quality/Reliability Technician. You're fairly neutral about who gets the new business. Both suppliers built a prototype that has consistently met the design specifications.

Precision Ax's record on quality hasn't been as good as you would like to see, but compared to some of the junk you get from other suppliers, they're not bad. In fact, you think they have a pretty good attitude about quality. Any time there's a problem, you notify your purchasing department and the next thing you know replacement parts are on the dock or Precision Ax's sales rep is in the plant reworking the parts for you. They will even reimburse your company if you want to rework any problem components yourself. You can't expect much more from a supplier.

Lazer Razer seems like a good supplier, too. You haven't visited their plant or spoken to anyone but their sales rep, but that's not unusual: in 11 years you've never visited Precision Ax either.

Quality Performance for Precision Ax Company

	1982	1983	1984	1985	1986	1987	1988	1989	1990
PERCENT Lots Accepted	96	94	94	97	95	94	96	95	95
PERCENT Assembly Line Zero Defects	88	91	87	88	87	93	90	93	89

Vice President, Manufacturing, Engineering and Purchasing. Quite frankly, you haven't figured out what you should be doing during the rehearsal since you haven't been involved with selecting suppliers or with the customer/supplier relationship up to this point.

While you're responsible for purchasing, you've been spending most of your time on what you consider key, ongoing engineering and manufacturing issues. You have a good background in those areas and through your leadership your company has been making continuous improvements and maintaining a competitive posture.

Busy as you are, you know that more needs to be done in purchasing. You see a tremendous opportunity since your purchased components represent 58 percent of your product cost. So you're making a commitment to improve supplier quality and the supplier/customer relationship. You're here to make a statement to your staff: you are serious about supplier quality.

You also know you won't be successful if you simply dictate what to do. You want to allow your people to work through the process in an open, participative manner. You want to create a climate where the group comes up with its own conclusions and feels ownership in the plan.

Your goal for today is to listen, to interject your ideas for the organization when you feel you need to, and to keep the group focused on the objective. Of course, you'll also add the top management perspective to the discussion.

How to Begin

After choosing your roles, your mission is to determine:
- ▶ The information to be collected
- ▶ The agenda for the supplier session
- ▶ Who will participate from your organization
- ▶ Who will be invited from the supplier's organization
- ▶ What role each of your representatives will play during the session
- ▶ What, if anything, you'll ask the supplier to do

Decide which supplier you plan to "rehearse" for, then go for it! At the end of the discussion, you'll be ready to tackle your own supplier quality issues. Good luck!

Index

AT&T 12
Cessna Fluid Power Company 125
Concurrent engineering 58, 62
Crosby, Phil 27, 35
Error Cause Identification (ECI) 71, 73, 75
Ford Motor Company 31, 33, 34, 36, 39, 118
Foreign competition 8-10
General Electric 12
Japanese Management Association 9
Long-term relationships 7, 8, 10, 11, 22, 35, 66, 67, 69, 131
Management involvement in quality
 process 2, 11, 27, 31, 33, 35-43, 50, 54, 55, 110, 114, 118, 124
Midwest Rubber Co. 39
Monona Wire Co. 15, 75, 78, 79
Motorola 12, 85
National Purity 8
Nonconformance Report (NCR) 71, 73-75, 103
Pareto analysis 49, 71, 75, 76, 101
Parker Hannifin 8, 37, 38, 41
Procurement Evolution Process (PEP) 20, 21
Prospect Foundry 62
Purchased components
 as a percent of product cost 7
 cost of quality 101
 reject rate 27, 32, 117
Purchasing's role in company 15-16
Quality
 measurement of suppliers 100, 104
 policy at Tennant 11, 82
 reporting 28, 41, 43

Quest for Quality 1, 27, 33, 39
Recognition 50-54, 117, 118
Reliability 41, 60, 85, 86, 91-95, 102, 104, 110, 116, 119, 129
Small Groups 48-50, 54-56, 62, 65
Solar Plastics...100
Specification development and review 86-88, 92
Statistical Process Control (SPC) 86, 89-92, 95
Supplier Corrective Action Request (SCAR) 77, 81, 110, 116, 119
Suppliers
     on-site assessment 36, 43, 59, 109, 112, 113, 118
     partners 7, 11, 22, 27, 66-71, 80, 132
     qualified 41-43, 109-112, 116-119
     quality goals 80, 82
     satisfaction rating 126-127
     sole source 8, 38
Training 2, 49, 50, 65, 68, 70, 77, 92, 129
Trojan Battery Co. .... .66, 67
Zero Defects Day 2, 33, 36, 38-40, 43, 50, 52